WOMEN in INDIA and PAKISTAN

The struggle for independ
from British rule

ROZINA VISRAM

CAMBRIDGE
UNIVERSITY PRESS

Published by the Press Syndicate of the University of Cambridge
The Pitt Building, Trumpington Street, Cambridge CB2 1RP
40 West 20th Street, New York, NY 10011-4211, USA
10 Stamford Road, Oakleigh, Victoria 3166, Australia

First published 1992

Printed in Great Britain by Scotprint Ltd, Musselburgh

A catalogue record for this book is available from the British Library

Library of Congress cataloguing in publication data

Visram, Rozina, 1939–
    Women in India and Pakistan: the struggle for independence from
British rule / Rozina Visram.
        p.   cm.
    Includes bibliographical references.
    ISBN 0 521 38643 8
    1. India – Politics and government – 1857–1919. 2. India – Politics
and government – 1919–1947. 3. Women in politics – India – History.
I. Title.
DS479.V57   1992
305.42'0954 – dc20   91-26093   CIP

ISBN 0 521 38643 8

Cover design by Joanne Barker
Maps by Jeff Edwards

Title page
Women demonstrate in the streets of Bombay against the arrest and imprisonment of Mrs Luckmani. She was being held for picketing a liquor shop in 1930. The procession is led by the daughter of the imprisoned woman (Popperfoto).

VN

For my parents

Acknowledgements

The author and publisher would like to thank the following for permission to reproduce material in copyright:
title page, 22*tr*, 22*br*, 28, 50*r*, 55*bl*, Popperfoto; 7, Mansell Collection; 9, 20, 22*l*, 37, 38, 50*l*, 51*t*, 52, 54, 55*tr*, The Hulton-Deutsch Collection; 11*r*, by permission of the Trustees of the British Museum; 11*l*, reproduced by permission of the Board of Trustees of the Victoria & Albert Museum; 12, City of Bristol Museum and Art Gallery; 13, 15, 17, 18, 19, 35, 41, 42, 45, 46, by permission of the British Library; 14, Mark Edwards/Still Pictures; 33, Mary Evans Picture Library; 43, Illustrated London News Photo Library; 51*bl*, 51*br*, *The Hindu*; 55*tl*, © PANA/Fotomedia; 55*br*, © Bangladesh High Commission/Fotomedia
Every effort has been made to reach copyright holders; the publishers would be glad to hear from anyone whose rights they have unknowingly infringed.

Author's note

I would like to thank the following for all their help and support: the staff at the India Office Library and Records; the Fawcett Library; the series editors Carol Adams, Paula Bartley and Cathy Loxton; Dagmar Engels, G. Johnston and J. Ballantyne.

Cover illustration   Gandhi with the nationalist leader, Sarojini Naidu (The Hulton–Deutsch Collection)

Contents

Introduction

India under British rule, about 1900

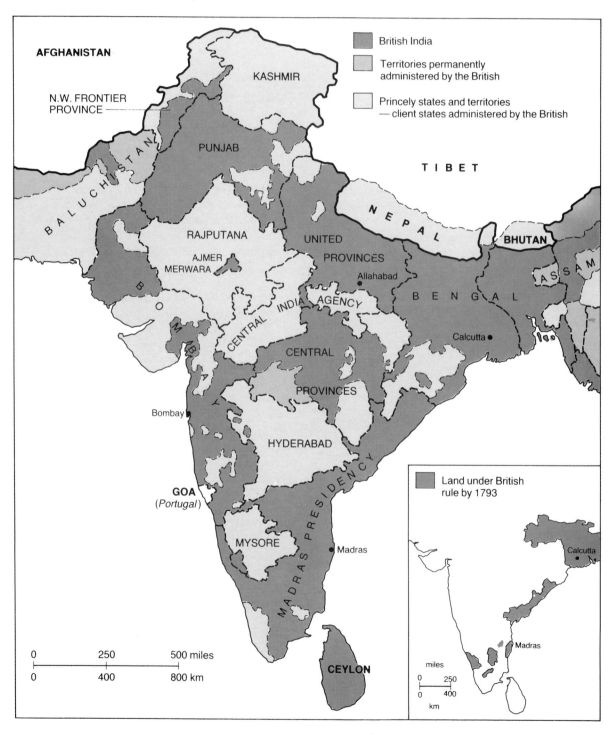

India under British rule

In 1600 the British East India Company began trading with India. Gradually, during the 18th and 19th centuries, the Company extended its control over India. By the 1850s the Company ruled most of India for Britain. The rest of India was ruled by Indian princes under British guidance. In 1877, Queen Victoria was made Empress of India, and British monarchs held the title of Emperor or Empress until 1947.

In 1947, after a long struggle against colonial rule, what had been British India became the independent nations of India and Pakistan. In 1948 Sri Lanka also became independent.

About this book

Until recent times most books on the history of the Indian struggle for independence from British rule told the story of men's struggle. We learnt about the part played by nationalist leaders like Gandhi, Nehru and Jinnah. Women, if they were mentioned at all, appeared merely as the wives, sisters or daughters of these leaders. And yet women were present at all levels of the struggle: as followers of Gandhi's non-violent campaigns, as vigorous and outspoken campaigners for self-rule, or as radical women who advocated revolution.

This book is about the role of women in the struggle for freedom in the Indian sub-continent. It describes some of the major events of the struggle and looks at some of the leading women. It tells of their involvement in politics, of how they campaigned for equal rights and for votes for women through the women's movement. It tells of the difficulties they faced, the hardships they endured, and of how their lives were affected in so many ways

The Viceroy of India is receiving a visitor. The population of India at the beginning of the 20th century was about 300 million. This vast population was governed by only a few thousand British officials. At the head of this government in India was the Viceroy, the representative of the British monarch. Notice behind him the large portrait of the Empress of India, Queen Victoria.

as a result of their participation. Whether women generally were politicised by their experiences, however, is open to question. Many women did participate politically, and some middle-class women took on political leadership roles in independent India and Pakistan. Yet, after 1947, many women went back to old traditional roles.

The sources

To write about women's involvement in the independence movement in India, without consulting archives in India and Pakistan, or personally interviewing women in India and Pakistan, imposes limitations. On the other hand, because India was ruled by Britain for most of the period covered in this book, it is possible to find several types of source material, both primary and secondary, in British archives and libraries.

Much of the source material available to us gives an account of the work of educated middle-class women in towns and cities. This does not mean to say that working-class women and peasant women were absent from the struggle: it is simply that their testimonies have remained largely unrecorded. Evidence about women from different regions, from different religious groups, and over different periods of time, is also uneven and patchy. Such evidence as is available reflects both the interests of the individual researchers and writers, and the absence of much primary source material.

Official Government records

Since India was ruled by Britain till 1947, many official Government records are available in Britain, most notably at the India Office Library and Records in London. These records consist of official correspondence between the Government in India and the India Office in London responsible for the affairs of India. They include reports, minutes, resolutions and policy documents, as well as records of Parliamentary debates. These documents do not directly record the work of women, however.

We also need to remember that evidence from the available official sources is presented from the perspective of the British rulers.

Autobiographies and biographies

Several women, as well as men, have written about their experiences, or have had biographies written of them. Autobiographies provide valuable information and give us a feel of the period. They tell us much about the actions, feelings and thoughts of the personalities involved. They do present problems, however. Some writers may write things to please their audience. Memories can also be faint or unreliable after many years. Biographies may also give a distorted picture, as they tend to be about the 'famous' or those considered 'unusual'.

Diaries and letters

Diaries and collections of personal correspondence, some in published form, can be found in record offices like the India Office and the Fawcett Library in London. These give us another view of the same events and so may provide a balance to the official sources.

Many women leaders corresponded with their families, and with the political leader, Gandhi. Others wrote to friends and women's organisations in England. These letters tell us of people's feelings and reactions, and show us what they considered to be most important to them.

Diaries, too, are an important source for understanding the experiences of women in the freedom struggle. They give us eyewitness accounts of what conditions were like at the time and may give intimate details of the writer's feelings and thoughts. For example, Vijaya Lakshmi Pandit's diary, *Prison Days*, which was published in 1945, gives us a valuable record of the campaigner's third term of imprisonment.

Journals and pamphlets

Various women's organisations, such as the Women's Indian Association, as well as political organisations like the Indian National Congress and the Muslim League, published conference proceedings and journals. These give us a record of their activities and concerns. But again care is needed not to generalise a complex situation. Not all women, or all nationalists, thought alike.

Photographs

Photographs are another valuable source for learning about women's involvement in these events. It is not always easy to find them as many focus on the male leaders, with women appearing only in the background. Some photographs, however, do show famous women leaders. These sources are important not only for what they portray, but also for what they leave out.

Gandhi (centre) addressing a session of the Indian Congress in Allahabad, 1940. Notice Mrs Pandit sitting on the right.

1 Women in Indian colonial society

South Asia today

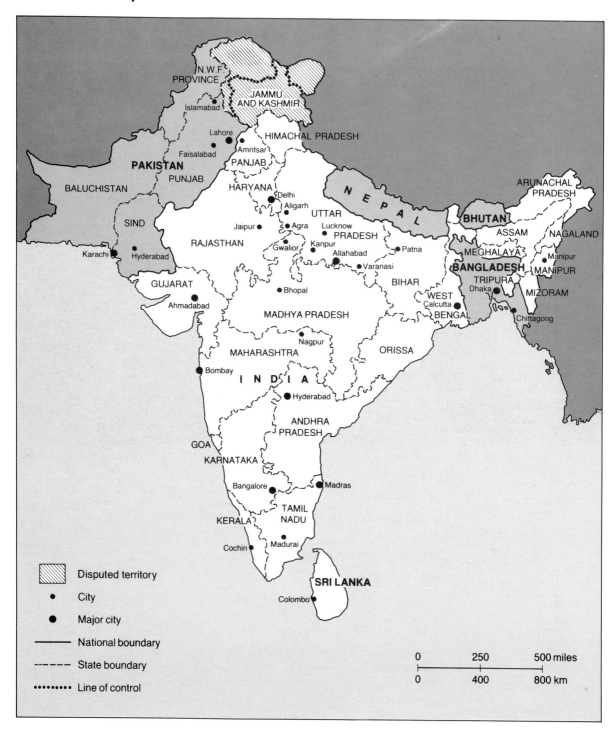

Disputed territory

• City

● Major city

——— National boundary

- - - - State boundary

••••••• Line of control

| 0 | 250 | 500 miles |
| 0 | 400 | 800 km |

Beyond the stereotype

The status of women in India has varied over historical time. It has been affected by conquests over many centuries, and by social and economic developments. Today the position of women still varies considerably depending on geographical region, culture, religion, social class, family background and caste. The 'patriarchal' system, for example, where the man is the head of the household, is not a universal practice throughout India. In southern India, in states like Kerala, the family organisation is 'matriarchal', which means that the female is the head of the household. Here women's position is more powerful, and they own property jointly with men.

Followers of the two major religions of India, Hinduism and Islam, have different attitudes to women too. Religious tradition and social customs govern Hindu and Muslim women's lives.

Traditionally, Hindu women could not inherit property. If widowed, they could not remarry. (It is still rare for a Hindu woman to remarry today.) Hindu women were also expected to wear veils.

Muslim women, in theory, enjoyed greater independence. They could conduct their own business. They could own and dispose of their own property. If a Muslim woman owned

(Above) *A Hindu lady worshipping at a shrine, 16th century.*

(Left) *A Muslim lady, Mumtaz Mahal, 17th century. She later married the Muslim Emperor, Shah Jahan. When she died at the age of 39, at the birth of her 14th child, her husband built the famous tomb, the Taj Mahal, in her memory.*

11

property when she got married, it remained her own. If divorced or widowed, Muslims could remarry without social stigma. But in practice, Muslim women were not always that much better off. This was because laws were interpreted and enforced by men. It was also the custom for Muslim women to wear *purdah*, clothing that concealed them when they went out (from *parda*, the Hindi word for veil).

Both the Hindu and Muslim male were protective towards women, and women did not enjoy economic independence or social prestige. Custom debarred them from public life.

Working women, Hindu and Muslim, in both rural and urban areas, were not so restricted by many of these social codes. They had to play their full part in earning a living so that they and their family could survive.

Campaigning to improve the legal status of women

During the 19th century the status of women in Indian society began to concern many. The British saw the low status of women as another example of the backwardness of Indian civilisation. Practices such as polygamy (having more than one wife at the same time), *purdah* and child marriage came under criticism. So did enforced widowhood and property laws which debarred women from inheriting property. Christian missionaries, who began arriving in India after 1813, and social reformers demanded that the British Government should reform Indian customs.

Indian intellectuals and social reformers like Rammohun Roy and Seyed Ahmad Khan called for reforms to improve the legal status of women. Many of them were influenced by Western education and a rediscovery of the greatness of ancient India and its learning. They campaigned for women's education and the removal of social practices that kept women down and which they believed did not exist in ancient India. As a result of pressure from reformers and a new phase in British administration, several laws were passed by the British in the 19th century to improve the position of women:

- 1802   a regulation made infanticide of female children illegal
- 1829   *suttee* (voluntary burning of a widow on the funeral pyre of her husband) was made illegal
- 1856   the Hindu Widow Remarriage Act legalised remarriage
- 1872   the marriage age for girls was set at 14 and for boys at 18, in an attempt to abolish child marriage
- 1870s   the Right to Property Act allowed Hindu widows a share in their husband's property

Rammohun Roy (1772–1833), an Indian reformer who campaigned for the improvement of women's position in society and against widow-burning (suttee)

The aims of the reformers were limited. They were concerned only with improving the position of women within the family, not with

Suttee *fascinated Western observers. This caricature of the practice by the English artist Rowlandson (1815) is called* The Burning System. *Many British missionaries in the early 19th century denounced* suttee *and Hindu 'superstition'.*

their position in society as a whole. As a result, only a small section of Indian women – those from the upper and middle classes – were helped. Working-class and peasant families did not possess property and so women from these families did not gain from the new property legislation. They were unaffected, too, by the law legalising remarriage as this was already a customary practice among the village labouring women.

The abolition of *suttee* was another example of legislation that only affected a tiny minority of women. *Suttee*, which literally means 'virtuous woman', was an ancient Hindu custom whereby widows voluntarily mounted the funeral pyre of their husbands, uniting with them in death. When Rajput warriors died in battle, for example, many of their wives sacrificed themselves in this manner. This was supposed to protect their honour and save them from the humiliation of surrender. It was not, however, practised widely – in some regions the practice had ceased altogether and it was unknown among the lower castes.

Economic life

Traditionally, upper- and middle-class Hindu and Muslim women led sheltered lives and were economically supported by their men. For example, most women, of all classes and religions, had very limited access to education, although in the late 19th century some educated women began to take up professions like teaching and medicine.

In many village communities, however, women played an important role in earning a livelihood for the family, producing handicrafts like baskets, hand-woven fabrics and pottery, and marketing vegetables and the handicrafts they produced themselves. Among the agricultural classes in most regions of India whole families worked together. Sometimes there was no division of labour, with men and women working side by side in the fields.

In some parts of India, even, it was women, not men, who controlled the household economic organisation. Indira Gandhi, the Prime Minister for most of the period between 1966 and 1984, describes what she saw in Manipur in north-east India:

13

Working in the fields: women farm workers weeding crops in the Punjab.

I remember my astonishment on my first visit to Manipur, at seeing that women not only worked in the fields and wove their textiles but dealt also with the marketing of their produce and occupied themselves with other important civic duties. What do the men do, I asked? They sit and smoke!

Indira Gandhi in Padmini Sengupta, The Story of Women in India

Social and economic change

As British power was consolidated in the 19th century, many changes took place which deeply affected the social and economic structure of India. Despite the reforms passed by the British, which, as we have seen, had only helped the privileged few, the result was an erosion in the position of women.

New laws governing property changed the matrilineal society of south India (in which descent was down the female side of the family) in favour of men. The gradual destruction of the Indian textile industry to the advantage of British cloth manufacturers destroyed women's economic base in the villages. New laws on land-holding and new taxes disrupted the old economic organisation and social order there. Many women, instead of working on the family smallholding or plot of land, were now forced to work as agricultural labourers or were driven into mines, or jute and textile factories.

Here working conditions were pitiful. An article in *Stri-Dharma*, the journal of the Women's Indian Association, described conditions in a textile mill in Madras:

[Women] attend the mill at 6.30 a.m. They do ten hours' work in the mill, return home in the evening at 6 p.m. to begin their household duties . . . Their wages on an average will not be more than Rs 10 per month, and with that amount they have to maintain a family of three, four or even five members. Their indebtedness is dreadful . . .

Stri-Dharma, *August 1928*

The position of women was not always helped by the attitude of the British Government or by the reforms introduced by them. Kamaladevi Chattopadhyaya, active in the women's movement, wrote:

14

Little do those who think that the emancipation of Indian women began with the coming of the British realise how successfully imperialism propped up a dying society and gave a fresh lease of life to obsolete traditions and customs under the guise of 'religious neutrality', and sought to perpetuate their slavery.

Kamaladevi Chattopadhyaya, The Awakening of
Indian Women, *1939*

It was therefore left to the women to voice their own concerns, and between 1880 and 1930 a women's movement emerged. Middle-class women formed political organisations with the aim of freeing India from British rule and improving the status of women in India.

Kamaladevi Chattopadhyaya fought for education and better working conditions for women. She was also prominent in the Civil Disobedience campaigns of the 1930s. In 1936 she joined the Indian Socialist Party.

2 Indian nationalism and the awakening of women

During the 19th century, male social reformers such as Rammohun Roy led the way in championing the cause of women. They campaigned for reforms to improve the legal status of Indian women. They set up schools for girls, founded associations for women and published magazines for women readers.

Women's social awakening

It was not long before educated women began to voice their own concerns. They put forward their own view of women's problems and attempted to find their own solutions.

In 1904 Bharat Mahila Parishad, the Ladies' Social Conference, was founded. This was the women's branch of the National Social Conference which had been established in 1887 to put forward ideas for social reforms. They discussed issues such as education for girls and women. The Conference met annually in conjunction with its parent body. In 1916, Professor D. K. Karve set up the first women's university, in Poona.

Pandita Ramabai, the author of *The High Caste Hindu Woman* (published in 1888), publicised the sufferings of Hindu women. A Sanskrit scholar, she had studied Hindu religious texts. She could see the contradiction between what was written in these sacred *vedic* texts and what had become Indian custom. She blamed custom for the low status of women. She also believed that women's status had been further worsened by alien British rule and its laws.

Pandita Ramabai's experience of the plight of women had been gained first hand, through her travels. After the death of her parents, accompanied by her brother, she had travelled extensively round India. Because of family poverty, much of this travelling had been on foot. In 1889 Pandita Ramabai founded a home for widows – the Sharda Sadhan. Here widows were taught skills so that they could become economically independent. She set up schools and a training centre for teachers, and also campaigned for medical schools to admit women for medical training.

The growth of women's organisations

In the late 19th century, women began entering journalism and publishing magazines for women. These magazines gave women a voice and provided a forum for women's issues. Swarnakumari Devi, the sister of the poet Rabindranath Tagore, who won the Nobel prize for literature in 1913, was the first woman editor. Her journal, *Bharati*, came out in 1884. This was followed in 1901 by the *Indian Ladies' Magazine*, published by Kamala Satthianadhan in Madras. The magazine came out regularly till 1918, and was restarted in 1927.

Middle-class women also began taking an active part in women's education and social work among village women. They did relief work during plagues, famines and floods.

As women gained experience they set up their own clubs and organisations. Many of these promoted both education and an interest in the welfare of the country, as well as providing a place for women to meet and exchange views. Between 1880 and 1930 many such organisations were set up in different provinces. For instance Swarnakumari Devi, the editor of *Bharati*, started the Ladies' Association, Sakhi Samiti, in 1886. Her daughter, Saraladevi Choudhurani, founded Bharat Stri Mahamandal, the Great Circle of Indian Women, in Allahabad in 1910. In 1914 the Begum of Bhopal founded the All-India Muslim Ladies' Conference at Aligarh. Papers on social reform and education were read at its meetings.

Then came the first India-wide organisation, the Women's Indian Association. Founded in Madras in 1917 by Dorothy Jinarajadasa, Margaret Cousins and Annie Besant, the WIA was a national organisation

Registered No. M-2435.

The INDIAN LADIES' MAGAZINE

Published Monthly

Vol. II   MAY 1929   No. 10

CONTENTS

Annual Subscription

Inland Rs. 5   Foreign Rs. 5-8

Editor and Manager
MRS. K. SATTHIANADHAN, M.A., Cannanore.

Assistant Editor
MISS P. SATTHIANADHAN, B.A.

A page from the Indian Ladies' Magazine, 1929. *The main aim of the* Indian Ladies' Magazine *was to forward the cause of women's education and to give educated women a voice.*

with branches throughout India. It had its own journal, *Stri-Dharma*, and its membership was open to all religious groups in India. It was the WIA which was to provide a voice for the women's campaign for the vote after the First World War.

The aims and objectives of the WIA

- To present to Women their responsibilities as daughters of India.
- To help them to realise that the future of India lies largely in their own hands; for as wives and mothers they have the task of training and guiding and forming the character of the future rulers of India.
- To secure for Women the vote for Municipal and Legislative councils as it is or may be granted to men.
- To secure for Women the right to be elected as members on all Municipal and Legislative councils.
- To band Women into groups for the purpose of self-development, education and for the definite service of others.

The people who belonged to these organisations were mainly educated women from all religious groups. They came from socially and politically conscious families and were supported in their activities by other members of their families.

Women's political awakening

Many women who were active in the women's movement also became involved in politics. They realised that there was no hope of raising the status of women while the country was under alien rule. They had no power to make their own laws. This could only happen if India was free from colonial rule.

Indian nationalists challenged the belief that British rule brought India many benefits. Peasants suffered under an increasingly heavy burden of taxes under British rule. Indians paid for the Indian army and for foreign wars in places such as Afghanistan and Persia, in which Indian soldiers had to fight. Indian agriculture and industries were developed to suit the demands of the British market for goods such as textiles and tea. Indians paid taxes, but they had no say in the government of their own country. The Indian Civil Service remained almost exclusively white; the examination for entry into it was held only in London. Even highly qualified Indians who managed to travel to London for the examination failed to get in. In fact by 1900, out of a total of 1,142 members of the Indian Civil Service, Indians numbered a mere 60.

Indians demanded justice. They asked for the reform of the economic system. They demanded a share in the government of their country.

Some women, too, began to challenge colonial rule, calling for a revolution to free India. Bhikhaiji Rustom Cama, a Parsi* from Bombay, was one of these. Born in 1861, she had been educated at Alexandra Parsi girls' school in Bombay and spoke several languages. Her husband was the son of the Parsi reformer, K. R. Cama. During the plague outbreak in Bombay in 1897, she worked as a social worker. She had also attended Congress sessions in India.

Madame Cama arrived in England in 1901, where she came under the influence of the Indian revolutionary movement. By 1909 she had settled permanently in Paris. She became active in socialist circles and made speeches critical of British rule at different radical gatherings. In 1907 she attended the International Socialist Conference in Stuttgart, Germany. In a fiery speech on behalf of the 'dumb millions of Hindustan', she denounced the 'terrible tyrannies' suffered by Indians under the British. She declared:

> Thirty-five million pounds were taken annually from India to England without return, and in consequence people in India died of poverty at the rate of half a million every month.
>
> *India Office Records, Home Political Proceedings, 1913. History Sheet of Madame Cama prepared by the Criminal Intelligence Office*

Madame Cama travelled widely in Europe and in America. Wherever she spoke, her message was the same – *swaraj* (self-rule) for India. She appealed to both men and women to work together for the emancipation of India.

In 1909 Madame Cama began publishing her own paper, the *Bande Mataram* (Hail Motherland). Copies of the paper, which she financed herself, were smuggled to India. Her anti-British literature and speeches, and her call for revolutionary means to free India, alarmed the British Government. In one of her speeches she advocated 'non-cooperation' – used so successfully by Gandhi. She said:

> They must desert and leave the English alone . . . They must not under any circumstances accept any offices . . . under the British Government.
>
> *India Office Records, Home Political Proceedings, 1913. History Sheet of Madame Cama prepared by the Criminal Intelligence Office*

She became a marked woman. Her mail was intercepted and dossiers were compiled on her by the police.

Madame Cama was known as the 'Mother of Revolution'. Several women students came under her influence, most notably Perin Naoroji Captain, the granddaughter of Dadabhai Naoroji, the veteran nationalist. In the 1930s, Perin Captain was a leading member of the Civil Disobedience campaigns.

In 1885, a group of educated Indian men formed a political party, the Indian National Congress. It pressed for more power for

Madame Cama (1861–1936). At the International Socialist Conference in Stuttgart, she made history by unfurling for the first time in public the Indian National flag that she had designed. It was a tricolour in green, yellow and red with the words Bande Mataram *(Hail Motherland) on the middle band.*

*A Parsi is a believer in an ancient religion which used to be spread widely across northern India, Iran and Turkey. Most Parsis now live in western India, particularly in Bombay.

Indians, and marked the beginning of an organised Indian nationalist movement. Membership of the Congress was open to women from its very beginning and women began to attend as delegates from 1889.

In 1889 ten women, mostly from Bombay and Calcutta, attended the fourth session of the Indian National Congress. The most well known included Pandita Ramabai, Swarnakumari Devi, and Kadambini Ganguli, a doctor from Bengal. After that, women in increasing numbers attended every session of the Congress. In 1917 the Congress elected its first woman president, Mrs Annie Besant, a political reformer from Britain.

Year	Number of women in Congress	Total %
1918	27	0.55
1919	74	0.90
1920	169	1.16
1921	144	3.00
1922	no information	
1923	60	3.61

T. Metcalfe, *Modern India, an Interpretive Anthology*, 1971

By the end of the 19th century many middle-class women had begun taking an interest in politics. They had begun to link the task of freeing India from colonial rule with their own emancipation. Certain events – the partition of Bengal in 1905, the First World War and the massacre at Amritsar in 1919 – made them even more aware of India's plight under foreign rule.

Boycott: 1905

The partition of Bengal led many women in Bengal into active political campaigning. Shudha Mazumdar recalled:

My first introduction to politics was in 1905 when I was seven years old and Mother served us with *phal-ahar* [fruit meal] when it was neither a fast day nor a *puja* [a prayer ceremony] day. It was not a holy day nor did I hear of any holy purpose, so I was somewhat puzzled to notice the unusual silence in the kitchen and find that no fires were burning at all. On enquiry I learnt it was associated with

the *swadeshi* [home-produced] movement.

Shudha Mazumdar, A Pattern of Life: The Memoirs of an Indian Woman, ed. Geraldine Forbes, 1977

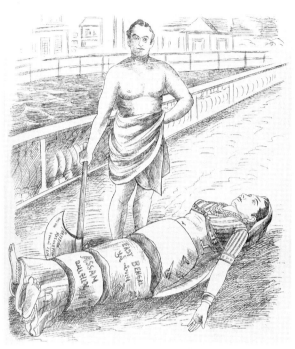

The Partition of Bengal, a cartoon from Hindi Punch, *July 1905. Lord Curzon, the Viceroy of India, is the person holding the axe.*

Bengal was partitioned in 1905 by Lord Curzon, the Viceroy of India. The British claimed this was necessary as Bengal was too big to govern as one province. The Bengalis saw it as a move to weaken Bengali nationalism. Public protests were organised and petitions were sent to the Government. But all these met with silence. When by the middle of 1905 it became clear that Lord Curzon was not going to be moved, Indians took action. They called for a boycott of foreign goods. They pledged themselves to buy and wear only home-produced (*swadeshi*) goods. In the words of the nationalist politician, Surendranath Bannerjea:

the dominating idea was to be independent of Manchester and the foreign market for our ordinary wearing apparel, our *dhotis* [loin-cloths] and *saris* [women's dresses] . . .

There was a cotton mill at Serampore on the Hughli [river], which had been in existence for some time. It was resolved to buy up this mill and to extend its operations . . . An appeal was issued. I was one of the signatories. The money was easily found, being largely subscribed by our middle-class people and even by our women-folk. The mill was purchased, extended and re-named. It was called the 'Banga Luxmi Mill'*, as a compliment to the gentler sex, who had shown a practical interest in the concern.

*Luxmi = Lakshmi, the Goddess of Wealth.

Surendranath Bannerjea, A Nation in the Making, 1925

As hinted by Surendranath Bannerjea, women played an important part in the *swadeshi* movement. As a symbol of protest, some women smashed their foreign-made bangles; others broke up foreign-made cooking pots. They gave up wearing foreign clothes.

In his novel, *The Home and the World*, set in Bengal during this period, Rabindranath Tagore's heroine, Bimla, patriotically declares:

As soon as the *swadeshi* storm reached my blood, I said to my husband: 'I must burn all my foreign clothes'.
'Why burn them?' said he. 'You need not wear them as long as you please.'
'As long as I please! Not in this life . . .'

Rabindranath Tagore, The Home and the World, 1919

A British woman, Mrs Ramsay Macdonald, who was on a tour of India with her husband, a Labour MP, later to become the British Prime Minister, noted:

a tremendous movement [was] going on amongst the women. We are fond of labelling the Indian aspirations as sedition when if they were amongst ourselves we should call them patriotist. This movement seems to be spreading as much amongst women as amongst men.

Modern Review, 1910, quoted in Manmohan Kaur, Role of Women in the Freedom Movement, 1857–1947, 1968

A British journalist, Valentine Chirol, wrote of the powerful influence exercised by women:

the revolt seems to have obtained a firm hold in the *zenana* [women's quarters] and the Hindu woman behind the *purdah* often exercises a greater influence on her husband and sons than the English women who move so freely about the world . . .
In Bengal even small boys of so tender an age as still have the run of the *zenana* have, I have been told, been taught the whole pattern of sedition and go about from house to house

dressed up as little *sanyasis* [men who renounce the world] in little yellow robes* preaching hatred of the English.

*The colour yellow has a religious significance for Hindus. Holy men wear yellow.

Valentine Chirol, Indian Unrest, 1910

The imprisonment of Annie Besant

One event which sparked off sympathy amongst women was the imprisonment of the nationalist campaigner, Annie Besant. Shudha Mazumdar recalled:

When Annie Besant was interned by the British Government for stirring up the Indian people by her matchless oratory, and then on release had presided over the 1917 session of the Indian National Congress, I had trembled with excitement. Her words, 'to see India free, to see her hold up her head among the nations, to see her sons and daughters respected everywhere, to see her worthy of her mighty past engaged in building a yet mightier future. Is not this worth working for, worth living for and worth dying for?' thrilled me.

Shudha Mazumdar, A Pattern of Life: the Memoirs of an Indian Woman, ed. Geraldine Forbes, 1977

Annie Besant had come to India in 1893. She founded the India Home Rule League in 1916, denouncing British rule in her paper, *New India*, and in her speeches. She was considered to be a threat to the stability of British rule in India and was ordered to leave the country by

Dr Annie Besant (centre) among the leaders in the revolt against the salt tax, 1923. A noted English campaigner, she asserts that a stand against the salt tax is the beginning of the fight for home rule in India.

20

the Government of India. But Mrs Besant refused and was imprisoned. Indians rallied to her support and she was released. At the Congress session in 1917 she was elected president of the Indian National Congress.

The First World War and its aftermath

The partition of Bengal had affected people in Bengal personally, but the First World War affected many more in India as a whole. Britain needed all the soldiers it could get to fight in Europe, and India contributed about 1.3 million men to the war effort, for a cause that was very distant to them. India also provided skilled personnel, money and materials for the war. Many women worked for the war effort and many lost husbands, sons or brothers in the war.

After the war, the political reforms promised by the British did not come up to expectations. Self-government seemed remoter still. The Government of India Act, passed in 1919, gave the Indians a national Parliament which could deal with health, education and agriculture. But its decisions could be blocked by the British. Furthermore, the Rowlatt Act of 1919 gave the police wide powers of arrest and trial. To the Indians this was a denial of basic human rights.

Indians responded by calling for strikes and closure of shops. Violence broke out. In the city of Amritsar, on 10 April, two Indian politicians were seized by a British official. The demonstrators retaliated and the European quarter of the town was attacked.

The Amritsar massacre: 1919

Then came the massacre. On 13 April General Dyer, the military commander in Amritsar, fired on an unarmed crowd of men, women and children, gathered for a meeting in the city square. The death toll was 379 dead with 1,200 wounded.

Martial law was imposed, and the city was made to pay further for the attack on the Europeans on 10 April. Many women suffered humiliations. The evidence collected by the committee of inquiry of the Indian National Congress included accounts such as this:

> Reaching the village, he [the British officer in charge] went round the lanes, and ordered all women to come out of their houses, himself forcing them out with sticks. He made us all stand near the village *sarai*. He beat some with his sticks and spat at them and used the foulest and most unmentionable language. He hit me twice and spat in my face. He forcibly uncovered the faces of all the women, brushing aside the veils with his own stick . . . He gave me a kick also and ordered us to undergo the torture of holding our ears by passing our hands round the legs while being bent double.
>
> *From Statement 362, quoted in Manmohan Kaur,* Role of Women in the Freedom Movement, 1857–1947, *1968*

The massacre made a deep impression on the people of India and strengthened their resolve for freedom. Sarojini Naidu, who had attended the debates on India in the House of Commons in 1920, wrote to Gandhi:

> It is vain to expect justice from a race so blind and drunk with power . . . The debate in the House of Commons shattered the last remnants of my hope and faith in the British justice and good toward the new vision of India. The discussion in the House was tragic . . . They see only the members of the coloured race . . . unworthy to govern themselves as do other nations of the world.
>
> *Quoted in Eleanor Morton,* The Women in Gandhi's Life, *1953*

Nationalism gathers speed

The years following the First World War and the Amritsar massacre saw a new momentum in the struggle for independence. Hitherto the Western-educated middle-class Indians and the wealthy landlords had been active in the campaign to free India. But now, under the leadership of Mohandas Keramchand Gandhi, it became a mass movement. Young and old, rich and poor, educated and uneducated, merchants and industrialists, labourers and peasants, the higher castes and the *harijans* (literally 'blessed ones', Gandhi's name for the Untouchables), all joined together to rid India of British rule.

There was another change. Women now came in their thousands to join Gandhi's campaign of Civil Disobedience. They were not just women from educated middle-class political families, but women from all classes.

3 Women and the campaign of Civil Disobedience

The influence of Gandhi

Gandhi studied law in London. After qualifying he went to South Africa, where he practised as a lawyer. Here he supported the Indian community's struggle against the harsh South African legislation which denied them basic freedoms.

Gandhi returned to India in 1915 and joined the Congress nationalists. Indian poverty and the effects of British rule on India led him to champion the cause of the masses. He had soon transformed the nationalist struggle from a campaign of the elite into a mass movement.

Gandhi was not simply a political leader. He preached *satyagraha* (soul force), self-control and a simple life-style. He preached 'non-cooperation' with the British Government in an effort to paralyse the Raj and win self-rule.

'I hold the British rule in India to be a curse. It has impoverished millions by a system of exploitation and by ruinously expensive military and civil administration. It has reduced us politically to serfdom . . . Nothing but organised non-violence can check the organised violence of the British government.'

Gandhi, 1930, quoted in F. W. Rawding, Gandhi, *1980*

Gandhi as a young man.

Gandhi speaking to a gathering of women on the lawn of Dr Ansari's house, Delhi, in 1931.

Nehru addressing a great meeting of women and urging them to continue their fight in the campaign of Civil Disobedience, 1930.

Percival Spear, a British historian writing in 1965, described the women's struggle for equal rights in the following terms:

> But the event which did more than any other single factor to speed the process was the Civil Disobedience movement of 1930–31. Feeling was then so strong that those already in public life joined Congress committees and took to organizing pickets for liquor and cloth shops, processions and demonstrations in addition to the usual Congress activities while many thousands came out of conditions of privacy and semi-seclusion to support the cause. Some of these were so ardent that at times, as in Delhi, they directed the whole Congress movement in an area until arrested. Many of them went to prison and as a whole they showed a discipline and devotion rivalling Gandhi's trained *satyagrahis*.
>
> *Percival Spear, A History of India, 1965*

We saw in Chapter 2 that women had already begun to take part in political activity, but in nothing like the numbers or the degree of involvement suggested by Percival Spear.

It was Gandhi who had given this new impetus to the freedom struggle. He saw the struggle for independence not merely as one of transferring power from the British to the Indians, but as a struggle for social equality. He succeeded in mobilising women and making them an integral part of his policy of passive resistance.

Gandhi and the role of women

Women were encouraged to join the *satyagraha* campaigns as a mark of their equality with men. Gandhi told women at the annual gathering of the Bombay women's society, Bhagini Samaj, on 20 February 1918:

> Woman is the companion of man gifted with equal mental capacities. She has the right to participate in the minutest detail of the activities of man, and she has the same right of freedom and liberty as he. She is entitled to a supreme place in her own sphere of activity as man is in his . . . By sheer force of a vicious custom, even the most ignorant and worthless men have been enjoying a superiority over women which they do not deserve and ought not to have . . .
>
> *M. K. Gandhi, Women and Social Injustice, 1942*

From his experience in South Africa, Gandhi knew that Indian women could be a powerful force and did not lack courage:

> To call woman the weaker sex is a libel; it is man's injustice to woman. If by strength is meant brute strength, then indeed woman is less brute than man. If by strength is meant moral power, then woman is immeasurably man's superior. Has she not greater intuition, is she not more self-sacrificing, has she not greater powers of endurance, has she not greater courage? Without her man could not be. If non-violence is the law of our being, the future is with woman.
>
> *Young India, 10 April 1930, in M. K. Gandhi, Women and Social Injustice, 1942*

Gandhi, therefore, actively encouraged women's involvement. In the kind of non-violent war he preached, he believed women could play the same part as men. Moreover, because he believed women had a greater capacity for endurance and self-sacrifice and a greater capacity to love, he believed they would make good *satyagrahis*. His message appealed to many. Aruna Asaf Ali, the famous revolutionary in the 1940s campaign, remembered Gandhi's appeal for her in the following terms:

> Gandhiji's appeal was something elemental. At last, a woman was made to feel the equal of man; that feeling dominated us all, educated and non-educated. The majority of women who came into the struggle were not educated or westernised . . . The real liberation or emancipation of Indian women can be traced to this period, the 1930s. Earlier, there had been many influences at work, many social reformers had gone ahead, it was all in the air. But no one single act could have done what Gandhiji did when he first called upon women to join and said: 'They are the better symbols of mankind. They have all the virtues of a *satyagrahi*.' All that puffed us up enormously and gave us a great deal of self-confidence.
>
> *Zareer Masani, Indian Tales of the Raj, 1987*

Kamaladevi Chattopadhyaya, whose politically conscious mother had been a great influence on her, also remembered the new understanding of freedom that Gandhi gave her:

> and from the time Gandhiji's leadership arose, I became much more attracted towards the political question. Before that of course I was reading so much about the other leaders and about the political question – I used to very

diligently read newspapers – but there was a difference in the message that he brought to me.

Until then, the whole idea of self-government for India meant replacing the British by the Indian, we would have our own regime. But he brought a new factor into this old question and that was, his interpretation of freedom was in terms of changing the life of the people.

Socially I was much more stimulated and perhaps I may use the word agitated: why there should be social and economic differences both, why there should be caste distinctions, why there should be poor and rich . . . And it was the first time he directed his attention to this question and I felt that here was the answer, that political change must mean also social and economic changes.

India Office Records, Oral Archives, MSS EUR R 87

Non-cooperation

When Gandhi launched his first non-cooperation programme in 1920, women responded to his call, swelling the ranks of the freedom fighters. They went from house to house to make collections; they donated their own personal jewellery to the fund for self-rule; they attended public meetings and marched in processions. Young students gave up attending schools and colleges to join.

Women publicly burned their costly *saris* and adopted the coarse white homespun cloth (*khadi*), even appearing at public meetings wearing it. *Khadi* became a badge of equality and a nationalist 'uniform', and Gandhi's wife, Kasturba, addressed meetings on *khadi*. Bi Amma, an aristocratic Muslim woman, the mother of the Ali brothers, Shaukat and Mohammed Ali, who were leaders of the *Khilafat* movement, went around addressing public meetings. She campaigned against importing foreign goods, advocating the use of *khadi* instead. She mobilised public opinion and preached for Hindu–Muslim unity. She had discarded the veil after the imprisonment of her sons.

In Calcutta Bengali women went into the streets to sell *khadi* and to preach against the wearing of foreign or mill clothes. Three of them, Basanti Devi, Urmilla Devi and Suniti Devi (all from the household of the Congress Bengali leader, C. R. Das), were arrested on a charge of obstructing the gentlemen of Calcutta by trying to sell *khadi*. Men and women rallied behind them.

In the Punjab, women addressed meetings and made speeches considered 'inflammatory'. Parvati Devi, another tireless worker, was jailed for two years for her speeches – the longest sentence inflicted on a woman during this period. In Bombay, in Lucknow and in Sindh, women went on marches and processions singing national songs and promoting home-spinning.

Swadeshi and spinning

Women encouraged each other to take up home-spinning. The following resolution, passed at a meeting of women at Dandi on 13 April 1930, illustrates this:

This conference is of opinion that boycott of foreign cloth is possible only through *khadi*, and therefore the women assembled resolve henceforth to use *khadi* only, and will so far as possible spin regularly and will learn all the previous processes and preach the message of *khadi* among their neighbours, teach them the processes up to spinning, and encourage them to spin regularly.

M. K. Gandhi, Women and Social Injustice, *1942*

The political message behind *swadeshi* and *khadi* was simple. Importing cottons from Britain benefited the British economy; it drained Indian taxpayers while profiting Manchester and Lancashire manufacturers of cottons. Giving up imported goods, therefore, saved India money. Spinning and *swadeshi* also had another appeal: traditionally, it had been the means of giving village women an independent source of income. But Indian village industry had been destroyed by the colonial economy. Spinning, therefore, Gandhi believed, would once again give women back their economic base. As he told a women's meeting in 1921:

For the middle class it should supplement the income of the family, and for the poor woman it is undoubtedly a means of livelihood. The spinning wheel should be, as it was, the widow's companion.

Young India, 11 August 1921, in M. K. Gandhi, Women and Social Injustice, *1942*

For women, *khadi* became a symbol of their

economic independence. It also became a symbol of ridding India of foreign rule by regenerating India's textile industry – an industry which the British had destroyed.

Swadeshi became the rallying cry and spinning came to be seen as a duty. Krishna Hutheesing, Jawaharlal Nehru's younger sister, recalled:

> Two hours a day were used learning how to spin; for part of Gandhiji's plan for making India self-sufficient was that we should make our cloth from our own cotton instead of sending it to the mills of England to be woven and re-sold to us. However impractical this return to cottage industry may have been, it had a strong emotional appeal for the Indian people; and the spinning wheel became a Gandhian symbol for freedom from British economic domination.
>
> *Krishna Nehru Hutheesing,* We Nehrus, *1967*

Liquor (alcohol) carried the same message, as revenue from the sale of liquor added to the British Raj's income. Men drank away India's wealth.

The boycott of cloth and liquor

Women were given the special task of picketing foreign cloth and liquor shops by Gandhi. They responded enthusiastically, forming picketing boards and committees. In Bombay, for instance, the Desh Sevika Sangh, a women's group, organised picketing, and the following advertisement appeared in the *Bombay Chronicle*:

> Wanted: 2,500 women volunteers for picketing liquor shops in the city of Bombay. 500 liquor shops in Bombay require at the rate of 4 women in 2 shifts of 2 hours each, 200 women for regular picketing and 500 more are wanted by way of reserve. Send your names at once . . . Signed on behalf of the Provincial Committee for prevention of liquor consumption.
>
> *Vijay Agnew,* Elite Women in Indian Politics, *1979*

Picketing was a disciplined affair, women working in teams of two or three. In some cases, as in Bombay, organisations were formed to direct and coordinate the campaign. Their strategy was designed to put moral pressure on the shoppers, and in most cases they succeeded. H. N. Brailsford, who was in India during the autumn and winter of 1930, described how women persuaded the shoppers. It reminded him of the suffragettes in London:

> As the day wore on, even in the European streets one noticed that in ones and twos Indian women were seating themselves on chairs at the doors of certain shops. They all wore graceful Indian dress, but their sari was of orange, a colour that has in this land its heroic association.
>
> Few entered these shops. You might catch a glimpse of the owner reading or playing chess. But if anyone attempted to enter, the lady joined her hands in supplication: she pleaded, she reasoned, and if all else failed, she would throw herself across the threshold and dared him to walk over her body. These women are known to fling themselves in front of a car, and lie upon the ground before its wheels, until its owner yielded and took back into the shop the forbidden goods which he had bought. But these were the exceptional shops which had refused to give the pledge to sell no foreign cloth and no British goods. Most of the Indian shops gave this undertaking, and where pickets were posted, it rarely happened that an Indian purchaser tried to defy them.
>
> *H. N. Brailsford,* Rebel India, *1931*

When Gandhi had called on the women to picket, many had not expected Indian women to be able to play this role. Mary Campbell, a temperance worker in India, described her amazed reaction in the *Manchester Guardian* of June 1931:

> I thought he had made a mistake this time that the Delhi women, so many of whom lived in purdah, could never undertake the task. But to my astonishment out they came, and they picketed all the shops in Delhi, sixteen or seventeen in number. I watched them day after day . . .
>
> That went on for some days – until the licensees appealed to the Government. The hefty policemen arrived with police vans and warned the women to go away. I thought those delicate sheltered women would give in now; they would never endure being touched by a policeman. But they did, and as fast as one relay was arrested, another took its place. Altogether about sixteen hundred women were imprisoned in Delhi alone. But they had done their work.
>
> *Quoted in H. C. E. Zacharia,* Renascent India from Ram Mohan Roy to Mohan Das Gandhi, *1933*

Picketing of stores was a great success: the Government lost precious revenue, a quarter of which was brought in by the sale of liquor alone. Picketing was therefore declared illegal and arrests of picketers took place. But the women were not deterred. They went to jail in their hundreds and there were always more to take their place. It has been estimated that 17,000 women were convicted in the first ten months of 1930.

There were not enough prisons for women. The police, therefore, resorted to various methods of terrorising women: they bundled them into police vans and drove them out of town, allowing them to return only after dark. Water hoses were turned on them and the police charged at them with *lathis* (wooden staffs with metal tips at both ends). They were fined. But the women stood firm.

A fact-finding mission organised by the India League (founded in England to fight for self-rule) arrived in India in 1932. Ellen Wilkinson, Monica Whately and Leonard Matters (all Labour MPs) with Krishna Menon, Secretary of the League, spent three months talking to Indians of every class, religion and political opinion. They also interviewed Government officials. Some of the testimony they collected dealt with the treatment of women resisters. They reported:

> ladies were arrested, taken into custody, then taken some miles away from their homes or places of arrest to island *chars*. Mr Neogy explained that 'there are small islands thrown up in the middle of the rivers of eastern Bengal, and these *chars* are in many cases uninhabited and full of jungle'. The ladies are left in these places at dead of night.
>
> Condition of India. Being the Report of the Delegation sent to India by the India League in 1932

Not only in Bengal, but in Gujarat and other provinces too, the police used this method to intimidate women. They also used threats, foul language and violence. In fact shopkeepers sometimes became converts to the cause because they did not like to see police in the markets ill-treating women pickets.

Another favourite method used to deter pickets was to give them the hosepipe treatment. The India League delegation learnt:

> In the city of Madras and elsewhere the police used to douch women pickets and volunteers with coloured water. The water hoses of the Corporation were used for this purpose and this 'hose treatment' had the effect not only of drenching people but of knocking them down.
>
> Condition of India. Being the Report of the Delegation sent to India by the India League in 1932

A policeman, F. C. Hart, recalled that the Indian sense of modesty gave the police an advantage over women demonstrators:

> On one occasion in Patna City a number of women laid themselves down on the ground right across the street and held up all the traffic. When the Superintendent of Police arrived on the scene he was at first nonplussed. If they had been men he could have sent in policemen to lift them out bodily, but he daren't do it with women. So he thought for a bit and then he called for fire hoses and with the hoses they sprayed these women who were lying on the ground. They only wore very thin saris and, of course, when the water got on them all their figures could be seen. The constables started cracking dirty jokes and immediately the women got up and ran.
>
> Plain Tales from the Raj, ed. Charles Allen, 1976

But despite police violence, fines and abuse, the women stood firm. Up and down the country, women from Hindu, Muslim and Parsi families, from middle-class and peasant backgrounds, demonstrated their commitment to the cause, boycotting cloth and liquor shops. Some even went as far as cutting down the sweet date-palm trees from which liquor was made.

The salt campaign

Gandhi led many different campaigns of Civil Disobedience in the 1920s and 1930s. The most famous of these was his 'Salt March' in 1930.

The salt levy provided the British Government with another valuable source of revenue. Salt was essential for preserving food and also helped give it more flavour. In hot climates it is also important for health. In the past people had made their own salt, but the British set up a salt monopoly, which meant that anyone buying salt had to pay a tax which doubled the price. It was illegal for anyone to make their own salt. The poor were hit the hardest, for although the tax amounted to about $3\frac{1}{2}$d (old pennies) a head per year, for the poor it represented four days' work.

On 6 April 1930 Gandhi launched his famous salt *satyagraha* with a historic march to Dandi – a village by the sea, 380 kilometres from Ahmedabad –to make salt. When Gandhi picked up a piece of natural salt, it was a signal for Indians all over the country to defy the British and break the law.

Gandhi had not included any women in the original band of 79 marchers. He did not expect women to break the salt laws. He hoped they would limit their activity to picketing. But women were not willing to be excluded from this act of defiance. They protested at this division of the sexes. The British campaigner, Margaret Cousins, wrote:

> This division of sexes in a non-violent campaign seems to us unnatural and against all the awakened consciousness of modern womanhood. In these stirring critical days for India's destiny there should be no watertight compartments of service. Women ask that no conferences, congresses or commissions dealing with the welfare of India should be held without the presence on them of women. Similarly, women must ask that no marches, no imprisonments, no demonstrations organised for the welfare of India should prohibit women from a share in them.
>
> Women of India, ed. Tara Ali Baig, 1958

It was Sarojini Naidu who led the march to the salt works at Dharasana, 150 miles north of Bombay. The Government, unhappy at the thought of having to deal with a woman, sent in the police, and the salt depots were fenced off. The marchers were surrounded; they could not reach the salt works. The police hoped that the marchers would give up and return to their homes. Instead, Sarojini Naidu ordered her fellow *satyagrahis* to sit down. In a letter to her daughter she described what happened at Dharasana:

> After prayer and songs and flag salutations and a benediction from *Ba* [mother], I led my army across a mile of muddy lanes to the vicinity of the salt depots and now the fun began. Lorry loads of armed police [under the charge of the Collector and District Superintendent of Police] with guns and *lathis* [sticks] and all sorts of lethal weapons blocked the way making a cordon. Very cleverly the Collector said 'We are

going to do *satyagraha* also and stay here as long as Mrs Naidu chooses to stay.'

> So I promptly sent for a chair from a neighbouring hut and have taken my seat in the middle of the road and ordered my volunteers to sit and all the pressmen are sitting and the crowds also along the road while the Collector and other officials are walking up and down behind the police cordons. There is a police saloon at the station I believe to take me away some time.
>
> Meanwhile someone has lent me a very 'holy' umbrella to protect me from the sun. I have sent for some magazines from my suitcase and my thermos flask. So I am rooted here for the present.
>
> The Bombay Chronicle, 26 May 1930, quoted in Vijay Agnew, Elite Women in Indian Politics, 1979

The Dharasana salt raid was not a one-day event. Between 15 and 20 May, at regular intervals, a party of volunteers, called *swaraj* soldiers, would make a quick raid on the salt deposits. Mrs Naidu had been arrested on 15 May, but then released. Then on 21 May, as arranged:

> A band of about 3,000 soldiers [*swaraj* soldiers] with implements to effect trespass into the compound, such as ropes, wire cutters and wooden planks, rushed forward from the north-east side of Nava Zilla . . .
>
> India Office Records, L/P&J/6/1998

In the end the police re-arrested Sarojini Naidu. She was imprisoned for a year. Dharasana became a symbol of defiance and women everywhere began to manufacture salt. In Bombay, Kamaladevi Chattopadhyaya, with a band of 15,000, planned a mass raid on the salt fields at Wadala. The police arrested her on the eve of the raid. The marchers carried out her wishes, and her seven-year-old son represented her by carrying her banner.

Many others not only manufactured illegal salt, but went into the bazaars to sell small packets of salt – an act which could earn them and their purchasers either a fine or imprisonment.

Usha Mehta, who ran the underground radio station in the 1940s, described how even old women came out to protest at the salt monopoly:

> I remember, during the Salt *satyagraha*, many women of all ages came out to join the

Civil Disobedience: women evaporating salt from the sea. They are making salt in defiance of the salt laws in the Court of the Congress Hall at Bombay.

movement. Even our old aunts and great-aunts and grandmothers used to bring pitchers of salt water to their houses and manufacture illegal salt. And then they would shout at the top of their voices: 'We have broken the Salt Law!'.

Zareer Masani, Indian Tales of the Raj, *1987*

Throughout the Civil Disobedience campaigns, in the streets of Bombay and many other towns, groups of men and women could be seen early in the morning, on their way to the temple, singing freedom songs, or *pheries*, to inspire people. *Prabhat pheries* were morning processions with chanting of hymns. H. N. Brailsford recorded his impression of the *pheries*:

> Every day began with its public ritual. The city prayed and sang. At dawn and even before it, from every street there issued a little procession of white-robed figures. All wore the homespun costume of kadi [sic] . . . had Indian drums or triangles; all sang rhymed songs and ballads . . . called for a boycott of British goods, and proclaimed a vow to win liberty or die. These little bands numbered ten or twelve persons, sometimes men, sometimes children, sometimes women. They set the keynote of each day's life.

H. N. Brailsford, Rebel India, *1931*

As *pheries* were meant to be religious processions, the Government was placed in a difficult position. However, as their popularity among the women grew, new regulations were imposed.

As the freedom struggle intensified, the Government retaliated with brutal repression. During the height of the Civil Disobedience campaigns of the 1930s, many people were arrested.

The treatment in the jails varied according to whether the prisoners were category A, B or C. Prisoners were classified by social class: educated and professional classes would be category A, while peasants would be category C. Many women found themselves imprisoned with criminals, rather than political protesters. Conditions in some prisons were terrible. The

Number of arrests for the year 1933–34

Province	Men	Women	Total
Madras	3,302	316	3,618
Bombay	13,833	1,017	14,850
Bengal	12,645	813	13,458
United Provinces	14,545	685	15,230
Punjab	1,764	121	1,885
Bihar and Orissa	15,609	411	16,020
Central Provinces	3,814	303	4,117
Assam	1,201	97	1,298
North-West Frontier Province	6,350	1	6,351
Delhi	992	82	1,074
Coorg	263	9	272
Ajmer-Merwara	310	30	340
Total	74,628	3,885	78,513

India Office Records, L/P&J/8/694

following statement was made in court by a Mrs Sonawala on 1 November 1930:

> I want to say something about the lockup in which we are kept for the last six days. I am in the lockup. I am given a very small room with a small *chokdi* [small drainage hole for urinating] in it. There is no sort of privacy in it. The doors cannot be closed and the room is open on the road side. Policemen walk up and down in front of the room. It is impossible to take bath, answer calls of nature or even change clothes without being seen from outside. There is no facility for taking bath. The room is not even fit for dogs and cattle. It is a great shame that you have to keep women in such places. There is no light also in the room.
>
> *Quoted in the newspaper,* Amrita Bazar Patrika, *in* Manmohan Kaur, Role of Women in the Freedom Movement 1857–1947, *1968*

Krishna Hutheesing, who was in jail for 13 months, served her prison sentence in Lucknow Central Prison as a category A prisoner. Even here the cells were bleak:

> There were no walls, only bars, and the only protection from wind-driven rain was a piece of canvas rigged over the bars. It flapped loose in a wind and we would huddle in one corner all night trying to keep dry, but we were always soaking wet in the morning . . . There was not even a cot in the cell, though we got cots later, for we were Class A prisoners – Class B and C had to sleep on the floor . . . The food was awful . . . Washing ourselves was a problem. The other prisoners did not seem to mind sitting

out in the open yard by the tap and pouring water over themselves from a jug; but somehow we could not get used to bathing in public.

> *Krishna Nehru Hutheesing,* We Nehrus, *1967*

The women were not deterred by fines, imprisonment or by violence committed against them by the police. Some even gloried in their self-sacrifice as the following letter from a widow at Gandhi's *ashram* (a place of religious retreat) in Sabramati shows:

> all of a sudden the police came down upon us with a shower of *lathi* [stick] blows. I came in for a big share of them, receiving several on the head, the arms, the back, and the face and the ears. Blood streamed out from a wound caused on my head, but I did not budge an inch and asked the sisters to sit down. Seeing that I would not be deterred, the *foujdar* [police sub-inspector] came and arrested me and handed me over to the police. I was taken, bleeding, to the police *chowki* [lockup] . . . It was on this occasion that I understood somewhat the meaning of *ahimsa* [non-violence]. I was quite fearless when the blows were coming down upon me, and I assure you I had no hatred or anger in me . . .
>
> *Letter written by Gangaben to Gandhi in February 1931, India Office Records, R/3/1/289*

Reaction to the women's participation

To many of the men, the participation of the women was something of a surprise. Some did not approve of it at all. Jawaharlal Nehru, who was Prime Minister from 1947 to 1964, described the typical reaction at the time:

> Most of the menfolk were in prison. And then a remarkable thing happened. Our women came to the front and took charge of the struggle. Women had always been there, of course, but now there was an avalanche of them, which took not only the British government but their own menfolk by surprise. Here were these women, women of the upper or middle classes, leading sheltered lives in their homes, peasant women, working class women, rich women, poor women, pouring out in their tens of thousands in defiance of government order and police *lathi* . . .
>
> He [my father] disliked, in his paternal and somewhat old-fashioned way, young women and old messing about in the streets under the hot sun of summer and coming into conflict with the police. But he realised the temper of the people and did not discourage anyone, not

even his wife and daughters and daughters-in-law.

J. Nehru, The Discovery of India, *1946*

Some men, inspired by Gandhi, encouraged or even 'told' their women folk to take part in the Civil Disobedience campaigns. Nehru himself was greatly impressed by his wife's actions:

> When I heard that my aged mother and, of course, my sisters, used to stand under the hot summer sun picketing before foreign cloth shops, I was greatly moved. Kamala [Nehru's wife] did so also, but she did something more. She threw herself into the movement in Allahabad city and district with an energy and determination which amazed me, who thought I had known her so well for so many years. She forgot her ill-health and rushed about the whole day in the sun, and showed remarkable powers of organisation.

J. Nehru, An Autobiography, *1980*

Newspapers condemned Gandhi for allowing women to be in the front line. They thought it was unchivalrous and placed the Government in an awkward situation. The *Indian Mail* in an editorial summed up the sentiment:

> [involving women] is a direct attempt to complicate the situation by bringing in the possibility of a clash between women and the police. Every nation is justly jealous of its womankind and no Indian could regard complacently the rough handling of his mother, sister or wife by the representatives of law and order.

Vijay Agnew, Elite Women in Indian Politics, *1979*

An annual report of the Police Administration considered that women were deliberately used:

> An increasing share of the work was taken up by women both because it was becoming more difficult to find male recruits and because the presence of women folk was calculated to prove an embarrassment to the police.

Annual Report of Police Administration, *Bombay, 1932, quoted in Manmohan Kaur,* Role of Women in the Freedom Movement 1857–1947, *1968*

Despite police protests to the contrary, they did not hesitate to use violence against women campaigners.

4 Votes for women

A nation consists of men, women and children, and it is not possible for one sex alone to legislate satisfactorily for the other.

So wrote, in 1921, Dorothy Jinarajadasa, the Secretary of the Women's Indian Association founded in 1917, in her book *Why Women Want the Vote*.

The 1920s and 1930s saw women in diverse campaigning roles. Women also demanded the right to vote. In 1909 some Indian men, the big landlords, were given the right to elect a few members on the Legislative Council.

We saw in Chapter 2 that women had begun to form associations like the Women's Indian Association (WIA) to improve their position in society. Women were also becoming more politically aware. They had realised that to achieve an improvement in the social and economic condition of women, freedom from British rule was essential. The right to vote was an important step in this struggle. The vote gave the people a say in the government of their country.

Leading Indian women began to campaign for the right to vote in 1917. In recognition of India's contribution to the British war effort in the First World War, Britain had promised 'reforms' which were meant to give Indians a greater share in the government of their country. Indians had already begun to demand this. Women, however, found that they had been left out of these plans for reforms, and so they began a campaign for the vote.

Why women wanted the vote

Women demanded the vote to have an equal voice in the government of the country and the right of equal citizenship. They argued that men formed only half the nation and that women's participation was vital for changing conditions in India. They had to have the vote in order to serve the Motherland:

1 People want to have reforms for 'Indians', but does not the term include Indian women as well as men? Women form half the population, and they cannot be so easily ignored, now that they are awake to their rights . . .

2 We ask for the franchise as our right, and not as something to be given out of grace. Men say 'Home Rule is our birthright'. We say the right to vote is our birthright, and we want it . . .

3 If women have political power, they can use it to improve their conditions. Education among women will spread rapidly if women have the vote. If a Home Ruler is asked 'Why do you want Home Rule?' he says 'Because we can improve the condition of India soon if we have power in our own hands'. Similarly we can improve the condition and education of our women and of India if we have the power to vote . . . The possession of a vote is the shortest route to gain power and efficiency, and men know that too well . . .

4 Indian women have an argument which their English sisters had not. In olden days, in the days of India's real greatness, women used to take part in State affairs, not only as rulers and philosophers, but village councils were composed often of wise women as well as the men of the village. Hence the idea of having the right to give their views on National questions is not new to Indian women, they are only asking for what they once possessed.

'Why Indian Women Should Have Votes', by Mithan A. Tata, in Stri-Dharma, *May 1918*

The battle for the vote 1917–28

The Women's Indian Association went into action to demand the vote when Edwin Montagu, the Secretary of State for India, arrived in India in November 1917. Montagu toured the country for five months. He consulted delegations on India's demand for home rule, but he only met men.

Seeing that women were left out, Margaret Cousins, an experienced British suffragette, applied for an audience with Montagu. A group of women planned to discuss women's education and social reforms with Montagu, but they discovered that Montagu only accepted political subjects for discussion.

Undaunted, Margaret Cousins wrote:

> I then circulated a couple of extra sentences about political rights or rather 'opportunities for political service' in the draft of the memorandum. I knew the women interested in the Deputation believed in women being equal citizens of their country, and they wrote agreeing to the additions; so the vote was claimed. But in my own heart I thought it would be a century before Indian women would understand, or be interested in political matters. I entirely under-rated Indian mentality . . .
>
> Margaret Cousins, Indian Womanhood Today, *1941*

The Deputation

On 18 December 1917, a Deputation of 14 women representatives, led by Sarojini Naidu, met Edwin Montagu, the Secretary of State for India, in Madras. The Deputation was well prepared. To make sure that they would be taken seriously, Sarojini Naidu emphasised women's political experience. The Deputation explained that they supported the Reform Scheme drawn up by the Indian National Congress and the Muslim League (set up in 1906 to look after Muslim interests). But because women were not represented in the Legislative Councils, their interests were neglected. They, therefore, asked:

> when such a franchise is being drawn up, women may be recognised as 'people', and that it may be worded in such terms as will not disqualify our sex, but allow our women the same opportunities of representation as our men.
>
> Stri-Dharma, *February 1918*

The women's Deputation marked a new phase in women's political awakening. Although middle-class women had already begun to take an interest in politics (as we saw in Chapter 2), this was the first time that they had come out in public to put forward their demands. They came to claim their right to participate freely in all institutions of public life.

But Edwin Montagu was dismissive of the Deputation. He did not take women's demands for equality with men very seriously. A note in his diary reads:

> We had an interesting deputation from the women, asking for education for girls, more medical colleges etc. One very nice-looking doctor from Bombay, Dr Joshi, was present, the deputation being led by Mrs Naidu, the poetess, a very attractive and clever woman, but I believe a revolutionary at heart. She is connected by marriage [she was in fact his sister] with Chattopadhyaya of India House fame. [India House in London was the centre of the Indian Home Rule Society, a radical organisation.] They asked also for women's votes.
>
> The woman who drafted the address, Mrs Cousins, is a well-known suffragette from London. Cousins himself is a theosophist [a member of a religious group], and one of Mrs Besant's crowd. Mrs Besant herself was there..
>
> An Indian Diary by Edwin S. Montagu, Secretary of State for India 1917–22, ed. Venetia Montagu, *1930*

It is not surprising, therefore, that women were left out of the Montagu–Chelmsford report of 1918. This report outlined proposals for an increased representation of Indians in the Government.

But the women were not put off. The right to vote was a matter of justice. Women argued that they had a unique and vital contribution to make as *women* in the political life of the country. Education, child welfare, health and economics all affected women and the home. Men and women, therefore, had to work together for the welfare of the country. Women were not usurping the power of men, as Sarojini Naidu argued:

> I do not think that there need be any apprehension that in granting franchise to Indian womanhood, they will wrench the power belonging to men. Never, never, for we realise that men and women have separate goals and separate destinies and that just as a man can never fulfil the responsibility of a woman, a woman cannot fulfil the responsibility of a man. Unless she fulfils the responsibility within her horizon and becomes worthy and strong and brave there can be no fullness or completeness of National life.
>
> Speeches and Writings of Sarojini Naidu, ed. G. A. Natesan, *1918*

Such sentiments, no doubt, won them the support of many Indian men.

The Southborough Committee

The women mounted a spirited campaign to convince the British Government. Public meetings were held by local branches of the WIA. Women lobbied the Southborough Committee, which had been set up to make recommendations on the franchise question. Petitions were organised and women submitted statements supporting their right to vote. Women also lobbied Indian nationalist parties. The Home Rule League, the Indian National Congress and the Muslim Congress all passed resolutions in support of women's right to vote.

But all to no avail. When the Southborough Committee reported in April 1919, it rejected women's right to vote. The Committee saw women's suffrage to be 'out of harmony with the conservative feeling of the country'. It opined:

> We are satisfied that the social condition of India makes it premature to extend the franchise to Indian women at this juncture, when so large a proportion of male electors require education in the use of a responsible vote. Further, until the custom of seclusion of women, followed by many classes and communities, is relaxed, female suffrage would hardly be a reality.
>
> Report of the Franchise Committee, *1918*

Women reacted strongly to the Southborough Committee's decision. This was a double injury. Women were being denied the right to vote, and once again Indian social customs were being used to justify the disenfranchisement of women. Britain appeared more interested in keeping the status quo – the British Raj – by appeasing its natural allies, the conservative sections of Indian society. Promises of 'reform' towards self-government seemed far away.

Women condemned the report of the Southborough Committee. Protest meetings in support of women's suffrage were held by the local branches of the WIA. Telegrams demanding the vote were dispatched. At a meeting in Bombay on 12 July 1919 the following resolution was passed unanimously and sent to England:

> This meeting begs to draw attention to the fact that women in Bombay Presidency and other parts of the country already exercise franchise intelligently in Municipal and other elections. It urges there is no reason to consider it premature for qualifying women to exercise higher vote and requires that their sex should not disqualify them.

> The meeting considers the postponement of this question a distinct grievance and the denial of due rights to women likely to deter their progress. It earnestly urges the government of India and the Bombay Parliament to recommend the question of removing sex disqualification.
>
> *Radha Krishna Sharma,* Nationalism, Social Reform and Indian Women, *1981*

Finally, in 1919, Sarojini Naidu, Annie Besant, Herabai Tata and Mithan Tata arrived in London to give evidence in support of women's suffrage before the Joint Committee of Parliament. They addressed public meetings in London and enlisted the support of British women's organisations. The Women's Freedom League and the Women's International League campaigned on behalf of Indian women. Indian men, too, came to their rescue. At the Joint Parliamentary Committee hearing, representatives from the Indian National Congress, the Muslim League and the Home Rule League gave evidence supporting women's right to vote.

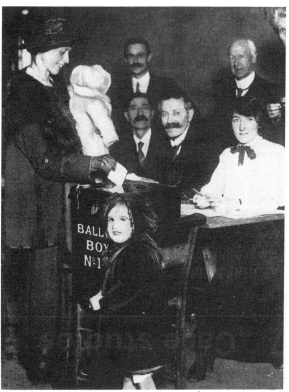

Women in Britain over the age of 30 vote for the first time in the general election of December 1918.

33

The Government of India Act: 1919

The campaign paid off. In 1919 the British Parliament decided that votes for women was a 'domestic subject'. It was left to the Provincial Legislatures in India, the law-making bodies in the various states and provinces, to give women the vote – if they chose to do so.

The Southborough Committee had declared that 'none of the local governments advised the extension of the franchise to women'. But it was proved wrong. Margaret Cousins gave her impression of the debate on the vote for women in one Provincial Legislature:

> Over twenty Members of the Council spoke. Not a note of opposition was heard . . . What an experience it was for me who ten years before had to undergo imprisonment because of the protest four of us Irish women then made in Dublin against the omission of votes for women from the Home Rule Bill introduced in 1913, to sit there and hear these Indian politicians, and to watch the record being made of a unanimous vote being given in favour of granting women the franchise.
>
> *Margaret Cousins,* Indian Womanhood Today, *1941*

Women gained the vote in Madras in 1920, followed by Bombay in 1921, the United Provinces in 1923, the Central Provinces, Bengal and the Punjab in 1926. The last to extend the vote was Bihar in 1929. Within ten years women could vote on the same terms as men, and be elected or nominated to Provincial Legislatures.

N. M. Dumasia, a member of the Legislative Assembly, proudly recalled:

> It is gratifying to find that in a country where men are accused of treating women as chattels, the political progress of women has been more rapid than in England and free from the war of the sexes and the smashing of the heads and windows which preceded the enfranchisement of women in England.
>
> *G. Forbes, 'Votes for Women', in V. Mazumdar,* Symbols of Power: Studies on the Political Status of Women in India, *1979*

Indeed, Muthulakshmi Reddi, nominated member of Madras Legislative Council, vehemently denounced the British members of the Provincial Legislatures for being obstructive in the franchise debates:

> The British government in my opinion and in the opinion of the majority of our public men and women, has not been helping our moral and social progress and has been adopting a policy of utter indifference, neutrality and sometimes direct opposition to all our social reform measures. Hence even we women have come to realise that a foreign government has no sympathy with the legitimate aspirations of the people . . .
>
> *Vijay Agnew,* Elite Women in Indian Politics, *1979*

The vote and the 1926 elections

Women had won the vote, but the franchise was very limited. Of the men 14 per cent were enfranchised, but a mere 1 per cent of the women received the vote. The reason for this was property qualification. Since few women were property holders, they were disqualified.

Women fared no better in the 1926 elections. Kamaladevi Chattopadhyaya and Hannen Angelo contested the elections with WIA support, but both were unsuccessful – Kamaladevi Chattopadhyaya losing by only 500 votes. However, Muthulakshmi Reddi took her seat in the Madras Legislative Council as a nominated member. Elected Deputy President, she became the first woman in this post. As a member, she performed her duties with zeal. She championed the cause of women and children. She sponsored legislation to abolish child marriage and to set up a children's hospital and training centres for poor women.

But women were determined to campaign for an increase in the number of women in the Legislative Councils and an increase in their voting strength. This proved to be a long struggle.

The fight for equal rights 1928–37

By the time the British Government began the next round of talks for 'political reforms' towards self-government, several changes had taken place. Frustrated at the slow pace of advance towards self-government, Gandhi had launched the Civil Disobedience campaign. We saw in Chapter 3 how women in their thousands had actively participated in the *satyagraha* campaigns. This earned them respect. The Indian National Congress, in recognition of women's contribution to the freedom struggle, passed the 'Declaration of Fundamental Rights' at the 1931 Karachi Congress. This outlawed sex discrimination, recognised the principle of equality and supported universal adult franchise.

Women had also founded two other women's organisations, the National Council of Women in India (NCWI) and the All-India Women's Conference (AIWC). These provided a further platform for women's campaign for the vote. The NCWI, founded in 1925 by Lady Dorab Tata, had as its main objective the improvement of the social, economic and legal position of women. It also had the wider aim of linking the Indian women's movement with the international women's movement.

The AIWC was formed in 1927 by Margaret Cousins and the WIA. Its aim was to provide a forum for debate on issues relating to female education and the welfare of women and children in general. A sub-committee was also set up to fight for women's voting rights.

Equal rights or special privileges?

Women's campaigns to have more women enfranchised formed part of the Round Table negotiations in the 1930s. Three Round Table conferences were held in London to find a way of ruling India which would satisfy everyone, and give the people of India self-government.

Demands for adult franchise were put forward at the First Round Table Conference in 1930 by Begum Jahanara Shah Nawaz and Radhabai Subbarayan. Both women were nominated by the Government to represent women's interests. Begum Jahanara Shah Nawaz wrote:

> We decided to ask for adult suffrage, but if that was not possible, to frame qualifications for franchise in such a manner that women should become a substantial portion of the electorate and should be given an effective voting strength.
> Moreover, we asked for reserved seats for women in all the legislatures for only two elections.
>
> *Jahanara Shah Nawaz,* Father and Daughter: A Political Autobiography, *1971*

Committee of the All-India Women's Conference (AIWC), 1930. The AIWC, like the Women's Indian Association (WIA), believed that freedom from colonial rule was essential for improving the position of women. Consequently the majority of its members actively supported Congress's satyagraha *campaigns of the 1930s.*

In the front row, from left to right are: Mrs Hamid Ali, Mrs Brijlal Nehru, Mrs P K Seu, Mrs Kamaladevi Chattopadhyaya, Mrs Sarojini Naidu, Mrs Hinde-Koper, Mrs Paridoonji, Mrs Cousins and Mrs Hamsa Mehta.

The Conference rejected the principle of adult franchise put forward by the women. Instead, it proposed to give the right to vote to wives and widows of men who were property owners. Although wifehood qualification was not a new device – it had been tried out in England – and would give more women the right to vote, many women, especially in the WIA, AIWC and NCWI, rejected it. As Muthulakshmi Reddi, the Vice-President of the WIA, pointed out:

> the elementary rights of a human being should not be based on some extraneous factor (such as wifehood) which is not under one's control . . .
>
> *1 May 1931, Rathbone Papers, Fawcett Library*
> *Collection*

The NCWI, AIWC and WIA also rejected reservation of seats. They were pledged to the principle of equal citizenship. In their memorandum 'Questions affecting the status and welfare of Indian women in the future Constitution of India' they demanded:

- Equal electorates, without privileges like reservation of seats for women;
- Equal rights based on adult franchise and no devices like votes for wives and widows only.

After their participation in the Civil Disobedience campaigns, women felt confident. As Muthulakshmi Reddi explained to the British MP, Eleanor Rathbone:

> The memorandum urges Adult Franchise for women and no nomination or reservations. You see that the younger generation of women are full of hopes and they do not want any reservation and are quite willing to fight elections on equal terms with men. A new spirit has come upon our women and in the present movement even old conservative women have come out of their homes. Therefore the WIA has also agreed to these proposals.
>
> *6 May 1931, Rathbone Papers, Fawcett Library*
> *Collection*

However, not all women in India or their allies in Britain opposed differential franchise and special privileges. Eleanor Rathbone, an Independent MP in Britain, believed that the British Government would not agree to the principle of adult franchise. It was too radical a demand by the Indian women. She therefore supported wifehood qualification. Radhabai Subbarayan agreed with this. She also supported reservation of seats for women. This, she felt, was the only way to give women seats in the legislatures. She believed that women

Cartoon of the Indian Round Table Conference, 1930–31. Notice the number of female representatives.

The Second Round Table Conference in London, 1931. Gandhi, the leader of the Indian Congress, attended, as did Sarojini Naidu as the women's delegate. Radhabai Subbarayan and Begum Jahanara Shah Nawaz were nominated members by the Government. Here they are walking along the quayside at Boulogne to the boat for England. The Conference did not reach any decision.

would not succeed in an open contest against experienced male candidates.

But the WIA and its allies regarded the principle of equal citizenship an important constitutional principle. They considered that special privileges would not give women the same status. Open contests would, on the other hand, allow capable women to be elected.

What kind of franchise?

Despite intense lobbying, evidence to the committees and petitions, women did not succeed in gaining adult franchise or equal rights.

The Lothian Committee on Franchise merely proposed:

- lower property qualification for both men and women (this would enfranchise 1,929,000 women);
- literacy qualification (1,265,000 women);
- wifehood qualification (4,306,000 women).

- 2–5 per cent of the seats on Provincial Councils to be reserved for women.

Under this scheme a mere $6\frac{1}{2}$ million women voters out of a total adult women's population of 70 million would be enfranchised.

Women were further angered by the 1932 Communal Award. This proposed the reservation of 3 per cent of the seats for women on a communal basis, based on the religion of the communities of India.

Many women felt betrayed. Radhabai Subbarayan, who had attended all the conferences and committees and who supported reservation of seats for women, articulated women's anger at splitting women on religious lines. In a statement to the press and in a letter to Ramsay MacDonald, the British Prime Minister, she wrote:

Indian women of public experience strongly disapprove of this proposal. As I stated at the Round Table Conference, they have all along refused to allow communal difference in any form to enter their movements. One of the main reasons for demanding reservation of seats for women was that such a measure would enable women to enter political life through a non-communal door. They are most anxious to have some method by which they could seek election to Legislatures as citizens and not as members of any particular community.

Subbarayan to Ramsey MacDonald, 23 August 1932, Rathbone Papers, Fawcett Library Collection

She was even more emphatic to Eleanor Rathbone:

Women have been making splendid progress all over the country and we fear that communalism among them will set their clock back . . . The interests of women and children in particular and of the country in general, for which they have been steadily working all these years, will surely recede to the background and women will be compelled to think of only communal interests. They will be puppets in the hands of die-hard communalists and think communally and act communally and their outlook will become narrow . . . With communalism among women we shall never be able to get the best type of woman in politics . . .

Subbarayan to Rathbone, 16 September 1932, Rathbone Papers, Fawcett Library Collection

Many Muslim women in the women's movement were placed in a difficult position. Fearing Hindu domination, the Muslim League had begun to ask for their interests to be safeguarded. Reservation of seats on a communal basis gave Muslims security. Begum Jahanara Shah Nawaz, who had attended the Round Table Conferences, was sympathetic. Begum Shareefa Hamid Ali, the AIWC treasurer, on the other hand, was strongly opposed to it.

By the Third Round Table Conference in December 1932, women's hopes of winning the vote as equal citizens had receded further. The British Government wished to avoid any expensive and complex device. It also wished to appease, and so gain the support of, conservatives in India who opposed women's public participation. The British Government also distrusted Gandhi and the Congress. In the complex political situation women were marginalised.

Rajkumari Amrit Kaur, who gave evidence to the Joint Select Committee of Parliament on Indian Reforms. Some women's groups questioned the ability of the WIA, NCWI and AIWC to represent all women's interests.

Rajkumari Amrit Kaur was the daughter of Raja Harnam Singh of Kapurthala. Educated in London, she was also a world-class tennis player. She was Gandhi's secretary for sixteen years.

The Government of India Act: 1935

In 1935 the British Parliament passed a law called the Government of India Act. It gave more power to Indians at local and national levels, but Britain still controlled India's army and foreign policy.

The Act gave women over 21 the vote in local elections or Congress provided:

- they owned property;
- they were literate;
- they were widows or wives of propertied men.

This Act enfranchised 29 million men and 6 million women, a ratio of 1:5. There were 41 seats specially reserved for women on a communal basis although women were free to contest other seats.

Elections under the new Act were held in 1937. Margaret Cousins described how women rose to the challenge:

> The women voters were so enthusiastic in electioneering and casting their vote for Congress that it was evident that the women of the masses, the women workers in the villages and towns were awake to their responsibility and their powers as enfranchised citizens using the vote as a direct means of securing self-government . . .
>
> In areas where women contested seats with men the Congress women candidates were extraordinarily successful. One woman elementary teacher defeated the Vice Chancellor of the University of her Province, and another, the simple little wife of a doctor, routed the president of the district, who had been the parliamentary member of that place for twelve years.
>
> M. E. Cousins, in Kamaladevi Chattopadhyahya, The Awakening of Indian Women, *1939*

Although the vote was granted, this table shows that the turnout of women varied from province to province. Not all women exercised their right to vote. Nevertheless, the general elections of 1937 brought 80 women into the legislature. India thus became the third country behind the USA (with 140) and the USSR (with 130) in the number of women legislators.

With the outbreak of the Second World War in 1939, the struggle for independence took a new turn.

The number of women who actually registered and voted in the first elections held in 1937 under the Act of 1935

Province	Numbers who registered	Numbers who voted	Percentage
Madras	1,523,248	479,278	31.5
Bombay	305,750	129,535	42.4
Bengal	896,588	46,758	5.2
United Provinces	494,752	95,553	19.3
Punjab	173,459	58,216	33.56
Bihar	215,490	17,037	7.9
Central Provinces and Berar	259,750	63,744	24.5
Assam	29,680	8,678	29.23
NWFP	4,895	3,498	71.4
Orissa	70,526	4,670	6.62
Sind	27,940	9,705	34.7
Upper House			
Madras	2,578	1,420	55.1
Bombay	1,637	923	56.1
Bengal	2,136	437	20.5
United Provinces	1,684	598	35.5
Bihar	882	594	67.34
Assam	559	512	91.57

India Year Book, 1945–1946

5　Rebel women

Thousands of men and women, inspired by Gandhi's politics of *satyagraha*, joined the passive resistance campaigns in the 1920s and the 1930s. But at the same time there were some Indians who were convinced that non-violent methods alone would not free India. Revolutionary activity surfaced in Bengal, the Punjab, the United Provinces and Bihar. Among these revolutionaries were a minority of women, the most well-known of whom were in Bengal.

Why women revolutionaries?

Women joined the revolutionary movement for many reasons. Some were inspired by leaders like Subhas Chandra Bose, known popularly as *netaji* (the leader), a radical member of the Congress in Bengal. Others joined because of their anger at British policy, or because of their patriotic idealism. Tara Ali Baig, a historian, described why men and women in Bengal turned to violence:

> The fight against the British took this form of terrorism in Bengal because there were a very large number of highly educated young people who were very frustrated because there were absolutely no job opportunities for them. The only thing for an educated young man in those days was to go into the police, the ICS [Indian Civil Service] or the law.
>
> There was practically no other outlet. So there was a great deal of frustration among educated young men and women who felt that it was only when we were independent that they would be able to have a life and that the only way to do it was by terrorism.
>
> *Zareer Masani*, Indian Tales of the Raj, *1987*

The deeds of the revolutionaries inspired many young women. The exploits of men like Bhagat Singh became household legends. In 1929, when he was tried for throwing a bomb in the Central Legislative Assembly, and hanged, many wept. Kalpana Dutt, one of the two women involved in a raid on the Chittagong armoury in 1930, remembered the impact of men like Bhagat Singh:

> The narratives of revolutionary deeds, the lives of Khudiram, Kanailal, Bhagat Singh, no doubt stirred us to the very core, teaching us to defy death . . .
>
> *Kalpana Dutt (Joshi)*, Chittagong Armoury Raiders Reminiscences, *1979*

Kalyani Das, another young university student, was also drawn to revolutionary activity, but for a different reason. She began as a passive resister, helping to found the Chattri Sangha (Female Students' Association) in 1928 in Calcutta. She had also organised and taken part in peaceful picketing, but she abandoned this form of protest when a peaceful demonstration of the women from the Chattri Sangha led by her met with police brutality. This convinced her that the revolutionary message made more sense:

> I had to witness the most painful and inhuman tortures made on young student volunteers at the gate of the Presidency College. We also went to Midnapore where inhuman atrocities were perpetrated on poor villagers.
>
> *Geraldine H. Forbes, 'Goddesses or Rebels? The Women Revolutionaries of Bengal', Netaji Oration,* The Oracle, 1980

Educated and sophisticated, many of these revolutionaries had been brought up on the patriotic literature of Rabindranath Tagore, Bankim Chandra Chatterjee and Sarat Chandra Chatterjee. They also read about revolutionary movements in Ireland, Italy and Russia. Stirred by patriotic ideals, they wanted to strike at the British Raj and inspire the masses by their courage and sacrifices for the Motherland.

Many young women in Bengal, between the ages of 16 and 30, came under the influence of the revolutionary movement. They joined physical culture clubs and patriotic societies like Deepali Sangha (Enlightened Torch-bearers' Association) in Dacca and Chattri Sangha in Calcutta. They received training in physical fitness, and instruction in shooting, *lathi* and sword fighting.

Women who joined these revolutionary societies were given the same training as men. They carried out similar missions, smuggling banned literature and acting as messengers. They helped to manufacture bombs and they smuggled weapons. They sheltered fellow revolutionaries on the run, they carried out assassinations, and they organised and led attacks on British officials and buildings.

Revolutionaries in action

Idealistic young girls and women carried out terrorist acts. In December 1931, for example, Shanti Ghose and Suniti Choudhury, two schoolgirls from Comilla, assassinated the British magistrate. They had gone to see him on the pretext of getting his permission for a swimming competition. While he read the petition, the two girls shot him dead. They were only 16 and 17 at the time.

In February 1932, Bina Das, the sister of Kalyani Das, fired five shots at Stanley Jackson, the governor of Bengal, while receiving her degree at the Calcutta University convocation. Her attempt was unsuccessful. Bina Das, in her statement, emphasised that she had no personal feelings against the governor. But he represented the system which kept India under British rule:

> My object was to die and if to die, to die nobly fighting against this despotic system of government which has kept my country in perpetual subjection . . . I fired at the Governor impelled by my love of my country.
>
> *Vijay Agnew,* Elite Women in Indian Politics, *1979*

Bina Das was sentenced to nine years' imprisonment.

Another young revolutionary, Pritilata Waddedar, a teacher, led a dramatic raid on a club in Chittagong. This was the Pahartali Railway Officers' Club, where British officers and their wives gathered every Saturday evening for drinks and dancing. On the night of 24 September 1932, under the leadership of Pritilata, a group of 15 young men entered the club and began shooting. Confusion followed:

> The music, laughter and revelry came to a dead stop suddenly about 9 o'clock in the night.

> Instead there was a sound of bombs exploding and shots being fired. Those inside tried to get out by the windows, but then rushed back again in panic. Within a quarter of an hour it was all over – there was silence. Only the wounded groaned in pain and fear.
>
> *Kalpana Dutt (Joshi),* Chittagong Armoury Raiders Reminiscences, *1979*

A dozen people were injured, and one woman died. In the cover of darkness the raiders made their escape – except for Pritilata. She died a hundred yards from the Club having swallowed potassium cyanide. She was only 21.

The attack on the Chittagong armoury: 1930

The most organised attempt at an armed

Revolutionary: Pritilata Waddedar. Her father had lost his job after he complained about an English officer's rudeness. In 1932 she led a violent raid on a British officers' club in Chittagong.

uprising took place on the anniversary of the 1916 Irish Rising. On 18 April 1930 an armed group of revolutionaries, which included two women in their ranks, marched on the armoury in Chittagong. The officials were taken by surprise. The revolutionaries captured the armoury and seized the town. They cut all communications and proclaimed an independent Revolutionary Republic.

Kalpana Dutt, one of the two women raiders, described the momentous events in her *Reminiscences*:

> On 18 April 1930 a batch of armed revolutionaries raided the Chittagong armoury, burnt the police lines, put the telegraph office out of order, removed rails from the railway tracks. The word went round: 'Ananta Singh's lads have done it again!'
>
> *Kalpana Dutt (Joshi)*, Chittagong Armoury Raiders
> Reminiscences, *1979*

But expecting the army to come after them, the revolutionaries moved into the hills, where on 22 April they were surrounded. After a pitched battle they were forced to flee into the forests. For almost four years they carried on a guerrilla campaign, with many villagers, both Hindu and Muslim, giving the rebels shelter and support.

Kalpana Dutt remembered that the Chittagong revolutionaries were under no illusion that the Government would send troops. But it was important to make a stand and set an example to young people:

> the patriots would die to a man in defending their freedom. In the annals of the struggle for Indian freedom this tale would be an unending source of inspiration to all, forever!
>
> *Kalpana Dutt (Joshi)*, Chittagong Armoury Raiders
> Reminiscences, *1979*

Kalpana Dutt evaded arrest until 17 September 1932 when, on her way to meet the leaders on the run, she was captured. She was disguised as a man, which aroused police suspicion. Kalpana Dutt remembered:

> At the time I was not an absconder myself, but a student in the fourth year science of the local government college . . . For some time past, the intelligence branch marked me out as a suspect, as being one likely to have come in contact with the revolutionaries. But the lack of

evidence against me baffled them . . .

> The authorities therefore decided to keep me in custody, as they were anxious to make a thorough investigation to make sure about me . . . The police became convinced that I too was a revolutionary and an accomplice of Preeti . . . So they sent me up for trial as an accused under Section 109 and granted me bail. This section is applied only in the case of those who conceal their identity for immoral purposes!
>
> *Kalpana Dutt (Joshi)*, Chittagong Armoury Raiders
> Reminiscences, *1979*

She was then instructed to run away. The police were still anxious to prove that Kalpana Dutt had concealed arms seized at Chittagong. They also suspected her of recruiting girls for the Chittagong revolutionary group, one of the most active groups in Calcutta.

As a fugitive on the run she moved from

Kalpana Dutt: one of the Chittagong armoury raiders. In 1933, at the age of 18, she was arrested and sentenced to life imprisonment: she was considered too young to hang.

village to village in the company of Surya Sen, the leader of the Chittagong group. In February 1933, he was captured and hanged. Three months later, in May 1933, Kalpana Dutt was arrested and sentenced to life imprisonment. She was only 18, and so considered too young to hang. In May 1939, following popular pressure from C. F. Andrews, Rabindranath Tagore and Gandhi, she was released.

Revolutionaries outlawed

The Government cracked down on revolutionary groups. Some were hanged, whilst others were tortured and imprisoned for life. Villages suspected of sheltering revolutionaries were burnt. Fines were imposed and villagers terrorised. An old Brahmin (high-caste) lady, arrested with her children for hiding revolutionaries, was tortured and jailed. Kalpana Dutt met her in prison and was shocked:

> As I was entering the female ward . . . a dark-complexioned middle-aged widow came running to me and asked me if I was a *swadeshi* . . . She would not let me go and followed me . . . babbling all the time about the police. Warning me against them she said, 'They might torture you, but even then you must not tell them anything; they might even threaten you with hanging, but you must never give way.' The police torture had made her a little demented . . .
>
> *Kalpana Dutt (Joshi),* Chittagong Armoury Raiders Reminiscences, *1979*

Police action against the terrorists succeeded in disintegrating the revolutionary societies by 1934.

Quit India Movement: 1942

With the outbreak of the Second World War, political activity was banned. Even peaceful demonstrations and protests became illegal. In August 1942, despairing of any advance towards self-government, Congress passed the historic resolution: *Bharat Choro,* Quit India. Gandhi demanded independence now, war or no war, campaigning under the slogan, 'Do or Die'. It was the start of the biggest campaign of non-violent protest yet.

The Government responded by rounding up the top Congress leaders, including Gandhi. Sarojini Naidu, Kasturba Gandhi, Kamaladevi Chattopadhyaya and Vijaya Lakshmi Pandit were among those arrested.

But all over the country people defied the Government. There was a tremendous upsurge as men, women and even children organised resistance in order to paralyse the Government. India became like one vast rebel camp as men, women and children poured onto the streets. There were strikes and closures as workers stopped work. Universities and schools closed as students went on strike and held demonstrations.

Vijaya Lakshmi Pandit described one of these student processions:

> I was under great strain. . . . About two o'clock in the afternoon I heard the tut-tut-tut of machine-gun firing . . . In front of the university the spectacle was a frightening one. A barricade had been erected, and before it were police and military facing a vast crowd opposite. The air was full of slogans: 'Quit India', 'Release our Leaders' . . . After the shooting of the student

Police have used tear gas to try to persuade female students to abandon their sit-down protest in the street, 1946. The girls are wiping tears from their eyes caused by the gas.

43

who was leading the procession, all discipline had gone to the winds . . . Seeing me the crowd doubled their shouts and demanded that I be allowed to join them. At last I was permitted to do so.

Vijaya Lakshmi Pandit, The Scope of Happiness. A Personal Memoir, *1979*

Women organised prayer meetings and marches. In villages they marched to police stations and law courts to hoist nationalist flags. In one village in Assam, a 15-year-old girl, Kanaklata Barua, organised a crowd of 500 men. Marching at the head of the procession, carrying the national flag, she led them to the police station, determined to plant the flag. But they were ordered back. Undaunted, she told the police that the station belonged to the people's Raj:

unless the *thana* [police station] officer and his men wanted to act as the servants of the people, they must clear out and allow the people to take possession of the place.

Bejan Mitra and Phani Chakraborty (eds.), Rebel India, *1946*

She moved forward despite orders not to do so and firing began. She was hit in the chest and died, but some in the crowd succeeded in hoisting the flag.

Others, like Amar Kaur and her friends, resorted to more unusual means of protest. She pulled the emergency chain on a train on its way from Lyallpur to Lahore. When the train came to a halt, she and her fellow passengers shouted slogans like, 'Inqilab Zindabad' (Long live the revolution) and 'Gandhi ki Jai' (Victory to Gandhi). They were arrested, fined and imprisoned.

Working underground

The Quit India Movement gave women the opportunity to take on independent roles as leaders. With the arrest of the top leaders of the Congress, some women went into hiding and took on the responsibility of directing and organising activities from underground. Aruna Asaf Ali, Sucheta Kriplani and Usha Mehta were among these.

These women saw their role in the underground as providing guidance and leadership, and keeping up the morale of

activists all over the country. They collected money and weapons, printed leaflets and organised their distribution.

In a letter to Maulana Azad written from 'somewhere in India' in January 1947, Aruna Asaf Ali and Achyut Patwardhan, her male co-worker, gave the following reason for their activities:

We all recognized the urgent necessity of providing some guidance to the vast forces that were being unleashed . . . The spontaneous response of the people to the Congress call to act as free men is the greatest phenomenon of recent history.

Yet once they had set their marching foot upon the path of revolt, they clamoured for effective and undaunted guidance. They asked to be organised to whatever degree the terror regime would allow. And their genius triumphed for a time, over all the machinations and force of the white man's Raj.

Bejan Mitra and Phani Chakraborty (eds.), Rebel India, *1946*

The underground leaders were helped by rich and poor, men and women, all over the country in many ways. For instance, Sumati Morarjee, later to become India's leading woman industrialist, helped Achyut Patwardhan, another Congress leader who worked from underground. She provided him with a different car every day, which she borrowed from her rich friends. Others gave money and materials as well as providing safe houses. The risks involved were great for both the leaders and those who sheltered them.

Life for the women in the underground was not easy. It was full of uncertainty and they were constantly on the run. Aruna Asaf Ali compared it to that of the partisans in France during the Second World War. Dodging capture, she recalled, could involve all manner of upheavals:

I'd just gone to a place in Bihar and thought it was far too secluded for anyone to know I was there. I managed to get a nice little place done up to stay there, because I was very sick physically and wanted a little rest. I was just about settled, when suddenly a person motored down from Calcutta to say: 'Leave this place immediately. The police have already arrived at the station and they're on their way here'.

He had a rickety old car, and we got into it. That drive I'll never forget – rushing away like mad, knowing that they were already perhaps chasing us, almost like a film chase. Suddenly we found a deserted temple, where I managed to hide. This fellow went away with the car; after he went round and saw that all was clear, he came back for me late in the evening. Then he took me to Asansol station to catch a train for Bombay.

At night no body would open their compartments; only one third-class compartment was open, and I jumped into that and found somewhere to sit.

Zareer Masani, Indian Tales of the Raj, *1987*

Aruna Asaf Ali evaded capture for four years despite a price of 5,000 rupees being placed on her head.

The underground leaders had to contend with a Government monopoly of news which meant the press was gagged and Congress effectively had no voice. One means of keeping in touch with the people was to put out news sheets, often distributed by students, and in Bombay the activists hit on the idea of an underground – or pirate – radio station. Usha Mehta, its chief broadcaster, was one of the small group who ran the radio:

It appealed to me immensely and I jumped at the idea and plunged into the movement in spite of staunch opposition from my father who being a government servant [he was a judge] did not approve of my idea and who wanted me to finish my education.

Manmohan Kaur, Role of Women in the Freedom Movement 1857–1947, *1968*

The Congress Radio began its first broadcast on 14 August 1942 with the announcement, 'This is the Congress Radio calling on 42.34 meters from somewhere in India.' The radio became the link between the people and the leaders. It gave them Congress views of events which the party activists had collected from different parts of the country, broadcasting messages and speeches from the leaders encouraging them to carry on the struggle.

Running the clandestine radio was a hazardous business under the ever-watchful eye of the Government and the police detection vans. Another nuisance was the Anti-India Radio, which tried to jam their broadcasts; new locations for transmission had to be found almost every fortnight.

To begin with, the Congress Radio came on the air only once a day, but then began broadcasting twice daily, in the mornings and evenings, in both English and Hindustani. The operation lasted for nearly three months, but then their luck ran out and on 12 November 1942 the police raided their location at noon and cut off their transmission. Usha Mehta describes those last moments:

When the programme was almost over, we heard knocks at the door. We, however, just carried on the programme. Three bolted doors had to be broken open before the hunters could happily pounce upon their prey . . . Our colleagues who were listening to the radio, did get the hint of our arrest when they heard the hard knocks on the radio. Thus the breaking open of the doors served as a call-sign on our arrest.

Bejan Mitra and Phani Chakraborty (eds.), Rebel India, *1946*

Usha Mehta was sentenced to four years' imprisonment for her part in running the Congress Radio.

Rani Lakshmi Bai of Jhansi: India's 'Joan of Arc'. She was the leader of the 1857 Rising against the British. The Rani of Jhansi became a symbol of female sacrifice and resistance to British rule. This portrait was painted in watercolour on ivory, soon after her death.

The Rani of Jhansi Regiment

Women living in east Asia demonstrated their opposition to the British Raj in India by joining the Indian Independence League, a civilian organisation formed in the countries of south-east Asia under Japanese occupation during the Second World War, and setting up women's sections. To begin with these women's sections concentrated on carrying out relief work, collecting bandages, funds and other materials needed for the Indian National Army (INA). But the arrival of Subhas Chandra Bose, the radical member of the Congress in Bengal, in July 1943 introduced a new spirit into the organisation. At a mass meeting of men and women in July 1943, in Singapore, Bose, a strong believer in women's equality, fired their imagination:

> I want also a unit of brave Indian women to form a 'Death-defying Regiment' who will wield the sword which the brave Rani of Jhansi wielded in India's First War of Independence in 1857.
>
> *K. S. Giani,* Indian Independence Movement in East Asia, *1947*

Women saw their potential as so many Ranis ready to drive the British out of India. The regiment was to become part of the INA.

The Rani of Jhansi Regiment was formed on 22 October 1943, in Singapore, as a volunteer force of 100 women, with Dr Lakshmi Swaminathan, a trained doctor, and Manoranjita Thavar in command of the regiment.

Some of the women who joined it had husbands in the INA, but the majority were young girls. Some even ran away from their homes to join the regiment in order to prove their willingness to help liberate India. Kantha Lakshmi was one of them:

> I was very anxious to join the camp from the very moment Netaji [Subhas Chandra Bose] opened it. Many a time I expressed my desire to my parents but they scolded me and threatened me. One day I told them that I would run away to the camp if they would not willingly consent and grant my only desire.
>
> *K. S. Giani,* Indian Independence Movement in East Asia, *1947*

(Above) *Inspecting the Guard of Honour presented by the Rani of Jhansi regiment in 1943.*

(Left) *Colonel Lakshmi, Commander of the Rani of Jhansi Regiment, saluting.*

But her parents refused. So Kantha Lakshmi ran away one night in January 1944 to join the regiment.

The regiment had two divisions – a fighting section and a nursing division – but the training received was similar in both. The day began with physical training, followed by military training. This involved the use of weapons, tactics, map reading and drill. In the afternoon the recruits were taught Hindustani, followed by more military training. Those who joined the nursing section spent the morning in a hospital, but after lunch followed the same programme as the fighting unit.

Women of the regiment dressed in soldiers' uniforms. They wore caps, shirts, jodhpurs, breeches and boots. Many cut their hair short. There was no distinction between the women's regiment and the men's regiment of the INA. The women were highly disciplined and prepared for war.

By 1944 the regiment numbered 1,000 women, spread over three camps at Singapore, Bangkok and Rangoon. The Ranis were ready and anxious to go on active service and appealed to Bose to let them go to the front and share in the fighting:

> It is you who taught us that there is no distinction between men and women. It is you who gave us training fit for men folk, have inspired us with courage and moral stamina required for actual warfare. We have received complete training. In these circumstances why should we not be sent to the battle front without delay?
>
> *Manmohan Kaur,* Role of Women in the Freedom Movement 1857–1947, *1968*

The first batch left for Burma in early 1945, but the regiment did not see active service as by this time the INA was in retreat.

After the War, Dr Lakshmi Swaminathan, in a last act of defiance, refused to surrender to the British. She was captured and the Rani of Jhansi Regiment was disbanded.

Rebel women and police repression

Because the Government saw the Quit India Movement as an attempt to sabotage the Government's war efforts, it retaliated with unprecedented levels of police harassment. If women suffered greatly during the Civil Disobedience Movement, they now met with new levels of indignities. Usha Mehta recalls how women joining the Movement suffered appalling brutality:

> The police were absolutely brutal in their attitude towards women, and even pregnant women were not spared. Women were victims of brutal *lathi*-charges. Not only were they insulted and abused, but many of them were even raped. One of them in Bombay, I know, was raped not by one officer but by officer after officer, including the British officers. She was a worker in one of the mills. She found it extremely difficult to return home, and she wanted to commit suicide. It was only with great difficulty that some of the Congress women could persuade her not to do that and take her home.
>
> *Zareer Masani,* Indian Tales of the Raj, *1987*

This was not an isolated case. Many women testified to police violence. A 25-year-old village woman, Basantabala Maparu, mother of one child, tells us how soldiers came to her house in January 1943:

> They caught my husband and sent him to a distance . . . three soldiers entered our house and approached me. They caught me and tied my mouth with a piece of cloth. The three soldiers forcibly committed rape on me. I became senseless . . . On regaining consciousness I felt a bitter sense of shame and again fell unconscious.
>
> *Bejan Mitra and Phani Chakraborty (eds.),* Rebel India, *1946*

Another, a 19-year-old woman, married with one child, reveals:

> On 9.1.43 last, about 9.30 a.m., a Police Officer – Nalini Raha – came to our house with a band of armed troops. They caught my husband and took him away, and forcibly committed criminal assault on me. I became senseless . . . This is the second time I have been criminally assaulted.
>
> *Bejan Mitra and Phani Chakraborty (eds.),* Rebel India, *1946*

Women were shocked at the attitude of the authorities to their plight:

> Mrs Bagde is a remarkable lady of courage and leadership. She also told us of an incident. . . . She said that one day she, worried by frequent

visits from white soldiers to her house in batches throughout the day and late in the night took courage and went up to the Deputy Commissioner and told him of her trouble. The Deputy Commissioner bluntly and heartlessly retorted, 'Who has brought these white soldiers? It's your menfolk, your husbands and brothers.'

Bejan Mitra and Phani Chakraborty (eds.), Rebel India, *1946*

Although women suffered greatly during the struggle for independence, many felt elated to have been part of that struggle during the Quit India Movement. Usha Mehta sums up her feelings:

I have no words to express my feelings. I really felt it was the golden period of my life. I just cannot express as to how I really felt. But that was a desire that I cherished for a very long time, for many long years and that desire was being fulfilled. It was something worth living for and worth dying for. So I could realise the exact meaning or the exact feeling of what Mahatma must have entertained when he gave us the slogan – *'Do or Die'*.

Vijay Agnew, Elite Women in Indian Politics, *1979*

6 India and Pakistan: towards equality?

India and Pakistan: independence and partition

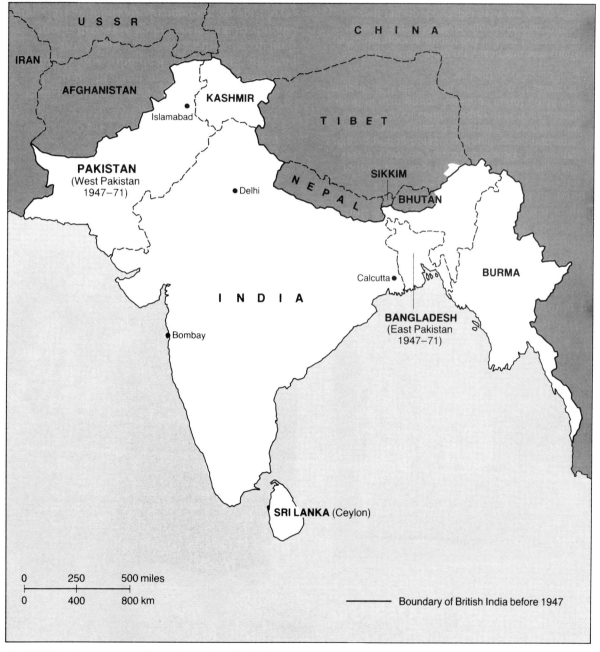

In 1947 India became independent from Britain. A separate Muslim state of Pakistan was created, in two sections, to the west and east of India. Later, East Pakistan fought a war of independence against West Pakistan. In 1971 it became independent Bangladesh.

Partition: 1947

With the growth of communal politics, tensions and conflicts arose among India's major religious groups, especially between the Hindus and Muslims. By the late 1930s, the Muslim League was no longer satisfied with various laws safeguarding Muslim interests within an independent united India. The League demanded a Muslim state of Pakistan. In 1947, when the British finally left India, two new states – India and Pakistan – were created. In 1971, what was East Pakistan became Bangladesh.

Independent India

The mass participation of women in the freedom struggle was an important factor in its success. The vital contribution of women had been recognised by the Indian National Congress as early as 1931 when the Congress, at its Karachi session, had passed the resolution pledging political equality to women.

The constitution of independent India of 1947 guaranteed political equality to women. The principle of adult franchise for which women had campaigned is enshrined in the constitution. It also guarantees women equality of status and of opportunity.

Many laws have been passed since 1947 to improve women's status and remove injustices. For example, the 1955 Hindu Marriage Act and the 1955 Hindu Sucession Act changed the legal status of Hindu women. The first legalised divorce and monogamy; the second recognised women's right to inheritance of property. Other legislation includes:

- 1961 the Maternity Benefit Act passed
- 1961 the Dowry Prohibition Act* passed
- 1971 abortion legalised
- 1975 equal pay for equal work introduced

*A dowry is a customary practice whereby a bride brings property and gifts to her husband at marriage.

(Above) *Gandhi meets the last Viceroy of India, Lord Mountbatten, and Lady Mountbatten, at the Viceroy's House in Delhi, 1947.*

(Right) *Nehru (standing on the left) meets Jinnah (on the right) in 1946. Jawaharlal Nehru, India's first Prime Minister, led the country from 1947 to 1964. Muhammad Ali Jinnah, a main figure in presenting Muslim demands, was founder of the new country of Pakistan in 1947.*

However, despite these laws, social realities have not been transformed except among the educated, for the mass of women remain ignorant of their rights. Even if they are aware of these, poverty and a lack of education means they are unable to seek redress. Social pressure to conform to traditional ways of behaving is another factor which contributes to the slow progress towards emancipation for the mass of women.

Gender inequalities persist. In education, in industry, employment and the professions women are outnumbered by men. Traditional attitudes to work patterns confine women to certain professions like medicine, teaching and secretarial work. Women have been prevented, by the lack of training opportunities and by illiteracy, from taking advantage of technological changes in industry and agriculture.

Three women delegates leave the new Constituent Assembly House after a session, 1947. Mrs Banerjee from Bengal is on the right.

In 1947, India became the largest democracy in the world. All adults, including women and Untouchables, were allowed to vote. Here voters are queuing outside a polling station in Tamil Nadu.

It was not until the 1970s that the Indian government made serious efforts to reduce the birth rate through encouraging contraception.

51

Country	Year	Age group	Rate of illiteracy					
			Urban areas			Rural areas		
			Total (%)	Male (%)	Female (%)	Total (%)	Male (%)	Female (%)
Bangladesh	1981	15+	60.9	45.5	78.5	83.5	70.9	96.9
India	1971	15+	39.6	27.6	54.5	72.9	59.4	87.0
Pakistan	1981	15+	53.1	43.1	65.3	82.6	73.4	92.7
Sri Lanka	1981	15+	6.7	4.4	9.2	16.0	10.7	21.4

Source: based on *Education in Asia and Pacific*, UNESCO, Bangkok, 1986

The vast majority of the population – about 80 per cent – live in the countryside, and the gap between women in rural and urban areas is marked. The quality of life of women who live in towns and who come from educated families has improved. They have been able to take advantage of the new opportunities: there are now women in Parliament, women working in the law courts and women teaching in the universities. But these are the exceptions. For the majority of women the gap between aspirations, legal requirement and reality is wide. Most Indian women live in villages, adhering to traditional values, and carrying out traditional tasks. The highest status an Indian woman can obtain is still motherhood, and preferably a son. The struggle for equality continues.

Independent Pakistan

The mass participation of women in the Muslim League occurred in the 1930s under the leadership of Muhammad Ali Jinnah. Jinnah encouraged women to participate in the League politics and to fight jointly with men for Pakistan. Speaking at the Islamia College of Girls at Lahore, Jinnah reminded women:

> I am glad to see that not only Muslim men but Muslim women and children also have understood the Pakistan scheme. No nation can make any progress without the cooperation of its women. If Muslim women supported their men, as they did in the days of the Prophet of Islam, we would soon realise our goal.
>
> *Parveen Shaukat Ali,* Status of Women in the Muslim World, *1975*

To increase enrolment of women in the League, a special Women's Committee was formed. At its session in Patna in December 1938, the League adopted a Special Resolution outlining women's equal role in the social, economic and cultural development of Muslim society.

Women became an important part of the Pakistan Movement after the League called for the creation of Pakistan at its 1940 session. Under the leadership of Fatima Ali Jinnah, Begum Shaista Ikramullah, Begum Jahanara Shah Nawaz and Begum Salma Tasadduq Husain, women mobilised themselves for Pakistan. They observed 'Pakistan Days', held

Muhammad Ali Jinnah, the founder and Governor-General of Pakistan. He died in 1948, just a year after winning independence. Here he is sitting at the opening of the Constituent Assembly of Pakistan in Karachi, the capital of the new state, in 1947. He has just placed two of the new national flags of Pakistan before his desk, and asked for comments from the members.

Between 1951 and 1958, Pakistan had eleven different leaders. In 1958 the army stepped in. General Ayub Khan became President until 1969.

women's symposia and distributed League literature.

During the 1940s, when the League launched a Civil Disobedience campaign in the Punjab and the North West Frontier Province, thousands of women marched in the streets of the big cities. They defied tear gas, police repression and *lathi* charges. Women planted Muslim League flags on public buildings like the Civil Secretariat and Lahore jail.

Women's role as equal participants in the birth of Pakistan was acknowledged in August 1947. Women in Pakistan, however, had a much more difficult task to get their rights recognised. This is because religion was the motivating force behind the creation of Pakistan. Conservative elements in Pakistan wished to mould the new nation according to their interpretation of an Islamic state. As such, the two women members of the Constituent Assembly, Begum Jahanara Shah Nawaz and Begum Shaista Ikramullah, encountered strong resistance to women's rights.

In 1954 the Charter of Women's Rights was finally passed. This recognised for women:

- equality of status
- equality of opportunity
- equal pay for equal work
- all the rights under the Islamic Personal Law

The legal safeguards under the Charter have not helped to raise the position of the majority of women in Pakistan society. In this respect the experience of women in Pakistan is similar to that of women in India. Women suffer from being disadvantaged in education, the professions, industry and employment. Custom and religious prejudice create barriers for many women. The gap between urban and rural women remains wide.

Women in politics today

In Pakistan, under the 1954 Charter, three per cent of the seats in the Central and Provincial Assemblies were reserved for women. Martial law in 1956 created a setback for women. However, in 1972, Zulfikar Ali Bhutto became leader and introduced a new democratic constitution which guaranteed equality of rights and privileges for all citizens of Pakistan irrespective of caste, race and sex.

The constitution contains further safeguards for women. Six seats are reserved for women in the Central Legislature, women can stand for elections in the general seats for the National Assembly, and five seats are reserved for women in each Provincial Assembly. These arrangements have guaranteed the presence of women in Pakistan's Parliament. Many women, like Begum Jahanara Shah Nawaz, Begum Shaista Ikramullah, and Begum Nusrat Bhutto have been prominent in Pakistani politics.

Women in independent India, too, have played prominent political roles. Vijaya Lakshmi Pandit was an ambassador for India. Rajkumari Amrit Kaur became President of the International Red Cross. Sarojini Naidu became governor of Baroda, and Lakshmi Menon was appointed Deputy Minister of External Affairs. Many women since have followed in their footsteps.

Commenting on the presence of women in high political office, Padma Desai and Jagdish N. Bhagwati wrote in 1975:

> One of the interesting features of Indian political life is the participation of Indian women. In this respect Indian society is almost certainly less inequitable than the Chinese, Soviet, and the American. Not merely does India have a female Prime Minister [at that time Indira Gandhi]. Women have also succeeded in becoming members of the *Lok Sabha* and *Rajya Sabha* [the two houses of Parliament], they have been governors and Chief Ministers of states, Ambassadors, members of the Cabinet and Deputy Ministers; and they have held the highest positions in the organisations of the major political parties.
>
> *J. N. Bhagwati, P. Desai, John Osgood Field, W. L. Richter and M. Weiner,* Electoral Politics in the Indian States: Three Disadvantaged Sectors, *1975*

Women have won political equality in India and Pakistan. Many have held high political office, but the actual number of women who get elected to the legislatures is not high. Men outnumber women, and women are disadvantaged when it comes to finding constituencies that will adopt them as candidates. But this is by no means a problem peculiar to India and Pakistan. Women in other countries have not succeeded either in being elected in large numbers to parliaments in their own countries.

Playing the kinship card?

Despite their small number in Parliament, women have been prominent in leadership roles. What has enabled women to reach high political office?

Women's experience during the struggle for independence, when thousands of women were mobilised, might be one reason. Gandhi's and Jinnah's encouragement brought many women into political agitation, many of whom continued in active politics. Political parties have continued to encourage women's involvement. But, perhaps, the vital factor might be family kinship and connection.

Independent India's ruling family. Jawaharlal Nehru on the left (Prime Minister, 1947–64), his daughter Indira Gandhi (Prime Minister, 1966–77 and 1980–84), and her son Rajiv Gandhi (Prime Minister, 1984–89). This photograph was taken in 1950.

Women leaders in South Asia

Every country in the Indian sub-continent has at one time been ruled by a woman. Democracy has developed in a particular way: politics are dominated by powerful families and dynastic links are all-important.

Mrs Sirimavo Bandaranayake, Prime Minister of Sri Lanka, 1960–65 and 1970–77. She was the first woman in the world to head a modern democratically elected government. She came to power after her husband was stabbed to death.

Mrs Indira Gandhi, Prime Minister of India, 1966–77 and 1980–84. She was assassinated in 1984.

Benazir Bhutto, daughter of former leader Zulfikar Ali Bhutto. In 1987, at the age of 35 she became the first woman premier of a modern Islamic state. She was educated in the USA and England; her Western upbringing made many Pakistani Muslims distrustful.

Begum Khaleda Zia, elected Prime Minister of Bangladesh in 1991. A widow and housewife, she was earlier married to General Zia ur-Rahman, who was killed by another army general.

7 Case studies

Sarojini Naidu
Indian National Congress

Sarojini Naidu: a leader of the women's movement and prominent in the Indian National Congress. She became the first Indian woman to be elected President of the Congress in 1925. In 1947 she became the governor of Uttar Pradesh.

Sarojini Naidu was born in February 1879 in Hyderabad as Sarojini Chattopadhyaya. In 1895 she went to England and studied at King's College, London, and at Girton College, Cambridge. After her return from England in 1898, she married Govindarajulu Naidu. This was an inter-caste marriage which symbolised Sarojini Naidu's ideal of a

non-communal India, an ideal that she stressed in many of her speeches. For instance, speaking to the students at a Historical Society meeting in Madras in 1903, she said:

> I say that it is not your pride that you are a Madrasee, that it is not your pride that you belong to the South of India, that it is not your pride that you are a Hindu, but it is your pride that you are an Indian.
>
> *Padmini Sengupta,* Sarojini Naidu: a Biography, *1966*

Sarojini Naidu was brought up in an atmosphere of nationalist politics. Her father had set up the first branch of the Indian National Congress in Hyderabad. He had taken the lead in advocating the use of *swadeshi*. Sarojini Naidu attended her first Congress session in 1904 in Bombay. Women's emancipation and other social issues – education, widow remarriage, the *purdah* system and child marriage – featured as major items of discussion. She also met Ramabai Ranade, the veteran women's campaigner, at this session.

By 1905 Sarojini Naidu had plunged herself into politics. At the Calcutta Indian Social Conference in 1906, she herself spoke on the education of women:

> Therefore, I charge you, restore to your women their ancient rights, for as I have said it is we, and not you, who are the real nation builders, and without our active cooperation at all points of progress all your congresses and conferences are in vain. Educate your women and the nation will take care of itself, for it is true today as it was yesterday and will be at the end of human life that the hand that rocks the cradle is the power that rules the world.
>
> *Lecture delivered to the Indian Social Conference, Calcutta, 1906, in G. A. Natesan (ed.),* Speeches and Writings of Sarojini Naidu, *1918*

By the time she met Gandhi in London between 1912 and 1914, she had already become a leader of the women's movement and had been active in the Indian National Congress, putting forward the resolution on the remarriage of Hindu widows in 1908. An inspiring orator, she was much in demand at conferences.

She supported the formation of the WIA. In 1917 Sarojini Naidu led the women's Deputation to Montagu for votes for women. At the Congress session in 1918 she put forward the resolution that men and women should be enfranchised on the same basis.

In 1919 she went to London to give evidence to the Joint Select Committee of Parliament on Indian Reforms. In her memorandum to the Committee she argued the case for women's franchise. While in London she addressed a meeting at Kingsway Hall in 1920, denouncing the massacre at Amritsar and the treatment given to women.

Her meeting with Gandhi led her into Gandhian politics of *satyagraha*. The Amritsar massacre and the debates in the House of Commons in 1920 had convinced her that India could not rely on British justice. Indians would have to redouble their efforts to win *swaraj*. She threw herself into the freedom movement, travelling widely in India to publicise the importance of non-cooperation, spinning, Hindu–Muslim unity and *swaraj*.

As an unofficial ambassador for the people of India she also toured the United States of America and Canada and visited Kenya and South Africa.

In 1925 Sarojini Naidu was elected to the presidency of the Indian National Congress. She was the first Indian woman to hold this post, but Sarojini Naidu did not regard this appointment as a novelty:

> In electing me to be the chief among your chosen servants . . . you have not created a novel precedent. You have only reverted to an old tradition and restored to Indian woman the classic position she once held in a happier

> epoch in our country's story: symbol and guardian alike of the hearth-fires, the altar-fires and beacon fires of her land.
>
> *Sankar Ghose (ed.),* Congress Presidential Speeches: A Selection, *1972*

She took a prominent part in the Civil Disobedience campaigns. In 1930 she led the march of 25,000 people on the Dharasana Salt Works. She was imprisoned many times.

In 1931, Sarojini Naidu represented Indian women at the Second Round Table Conference in London.

After the Quit India resolution of August 1942, Sarojini Naidu was among the prominent leaders of the Indian National Congress to be arrested. Her ill-health led to her release in March 1943. But a ban was placed on her freedom to speak. She complied with this for some time. In 1944, however, she decided she had to speak out against British propaganda that Gandhi was pro-Japanese. In her speech, published in the *Hindustani Times*, Sarojini Naidu ridiculed the suggestion that India would favour Japanese invasion:

> If any body has the audacity to continue saying it, it will be a lie. I can tell you authoritatively, that so far from being pro-Japanese we have been consistently against any form of foreign invasion no matter what label it may bear because we have had quite enough of foreign invasions. There are no two opinions among us on this.
>
> *India Office Records, L/P&J/8/625*

After India regained its independence in 1947, Sarojini Naidu became the governor of Uttar Pradesh. She was the first woman in India to hold this position. She died in office in 1949, a woman who had devoted her life to politics and the women's movement.

Margaret Cousins
Suffrage campaigner

Margaret Cousins: a key suffrage campaigner in England, Ireland and India. In 1927 she set up the All-India Women's Conference (AIWC).

Born in 1878 in Boyle, County Roscommon, in Ireland, Margaret Gillespie came from a large Protestant family and was brought up on Irish culture and Irish nationalism. She studied music at the Royal Academy of Music in Dublin, graduating with a degree in music.

In 1903, she married James Cousins, a poet. In 1906 they moved to Manchester, where Margaret Cousins attended the National Conference of Women and joined the suffragettes, led by the Pankhursts. Once back in Ireland, she played an active role in the Irish Women's Franchise League. She addressed meetings and took part in the stone-throwing and window-breaking campaigns in London and Dublin. She served several terms of imprisonment, both in Ireland and in England. When the Irish Home Rule Bill made no mention of Irish women being made citizens of Ireland, Margaret Cousins led the campaign to right this injustice. The experience she gained as a suffrage campaigner in England and Ireland was to prove of great value to her in India.

Margaret Cousins and her husband settled in India in 1915, where she involved herself in the Indian women's movement. In 1916 she was elected a member of D. K. Karve's Indian Women's University at Poona. With the foundation of the WIA in 1917, she became its general secretary, editing *Stri-Dharma*, the journal of the WIA, and organising women's activities at local, regional and national levels.

In 1927 she set up the All-India Women's Conference, a much more representative organisation of Indian women. The AIWC also established close links with women's groups in other parts of Asia and Europe. In 1931 Margaret Cousins took the lead to convene the first All-Asia Conference at Lahore.

It was Margaret Cousins who took the initiative in 1917 to organise the women's Deputation to Edwin Montagu to discuss votes for women. This marked the beginning of the campaign for women's right to adult franchise. Margaret Cousins wrote:

> Curiously enough, though I had the backing of some of the best women of India, I was the one voice publicly explaining and proclaiming the suffrage cause; not because I had any special fitness, but simply because the womanhood of India had not yet found its authoritative voice.
> *James and Margaret Cousins,* We Two Together,
> *1950*

After 1919 she became active lobbying in the provinces for women's right to vote. She organised campaigns to enable women to gain seats in the legislatures and commissions. She protested against the all-white Simon Commission and, especially, at the lack of any Indian women on it. She played an active role in public relations work abroad for Indian women.

During the Civil Disobedience campaigns Margaret Cousins supported the nationalist cause. She was especially critical of the Emergency Ordinance which restricted freedom of speech. In 1932 she was arrested and imprisoned for a year.

She was elected President of the WIA in 1933 and of the AIWC in 1936. In August 1943 she suffered a brain haemorrhage, which she never fully recovered from. She died in 1954.

Jahanara Shah Nawaz
Muslim League

Jahanara Shah Nawaz, as delegate to the Indian Round Table Conference in 1932. She was very active in the AIWC till 1947 and campaigned vigorously for a separate Muslim state.

Begum Jahanara Shah Nawaz was born in April 1896 in Baghbanpura, near Lahore, in the Punjab. Her father, Muhammed Shafi, was a lawyer and a founder member of the Muslim League in 1906.

Her father strongly believed that the Muslims were disadvantaged in India, dominated as they were by the Hindu majority. He campaigned for a separate political organisation and separate electorates to safeguard Muslim interests and cultural traditions.

Begum Jahanara Shah Nawaz came from a liberal Muslim family. Her father worked to improve the educational and social position of Muslims. He encouraged women's education and campaigned for their property rights. The women of the household wore no veil in public. Her mother worked for the advancement of Muslim women.

Begum Jahanara Shah Nawaz attended Queen Mary College in Lahore. In 1911, at the age of 15, she married Shah Nawaz, a nationalist lawyer, but she continued with her studies after her marriage.

She played an active part in the All-India Muslim Ladies' Conference. In 1918, at its Lahore session, she sponsored a resolution against polygamy which was passed unanimously. This is how she described the reaction of one woman:

> As I got down from the platform after finishing my speech on the resolution about polygamy, an old lady from the audience, with tears running down her cheeks, came and embraced me, and said that she was proud to be alive on a day when such troubles and difficulties of women were being discussed on responsible platforms.
>
> *Jahanara Shah Nawaz*, Father and Daughter: a Political Autobiography, *1971*

She also published a pamphlet explaining the need for such a resolution.

After the women's Deputation to Montagu, Begum Jahanara Shah Nawaz organised a women's committee in Simla to campaign for women's right to vote.

When the AIWC was founded, she attended the Conference as an elected delegate from the Punjab. She took an active part in the AIWC till 1947, serving as president of the provincial branch for many years and being elected Vice-President in 1932. At the same time, she carried on working for the All-India Muslim Ladies' Conference, believing that it was essential for Muslim women to have an association of their own.

She was elected member of the Lahore Municipal Corporation in 1931, serving on several hospital, maternity and child welfare committees and setting up health centres for women and children. She represented India on the Women and Children's Committee of the League of Nations and at the International Labour Conference in 1935.

In 1930, Begum Jahanara Shah Nawaz was invited by the British Government to serve on the First Round Table Conference called to formulate proposals for reform. She also served on the Second Round Table Conference in 1931 and was the only woman delegate at the Third Round Table Conference in November 1932. As a representative of Indian women on the Round Table Conferences, Begum Jahanara Shah Nawaz campaigned for women to have an effective voting strength.

She welcomed the Communal Award of 1932 (see page 37). By this time, like her father, she too had come to believe that Muslim interests must be safeguarded in an independent India.

In 1933 she was nominated as the member of the Indian delegation to the Joint Select Committee, on which she worked hard to gain the support of women members of Parliament and other prominent women for Indian women's franchise demands.

Begum Jahanara Shah Nawaz was elected to the Punjab Legislative Council in 1937 and was appointed Parliamentary Secretary in charge of Education, Medical Relief and Public Health. Getting Muslim women to vote had not been easy. She wrote:

> The Muslim women's seats were to be filled by separate electorates, and in the Punjab and Bengal they were to be elected by women voters only. It had been an uphill task to secure an effective number of women voters, when even the Muslim witnesses before the Joint Select Committee had opposed a special qualification for women.
>
> *Jahanara Shah Nawaz,* Father and Daughter: a Political Autobiography, *1971*

She was appointed to the Women's Central Sub-Committee of the All-India Muslim League in 1938. Between 1940, when the Pakistan resolution was passed, and 1947 Begum Jahanara Shah Nawaz played an important role in the campaign for a separate Muslim state. She addressed many meetings all over India, explaining and calling for the Muslim majority provinces to be included in the new nation of Pakistan. She marched with women in support of Pakistan and was arrested along with other Muslim League leaders in 1947.

In 1946 she was elected to the Punjab Assembly. She was asked by Jinnah to go to the United States on a good-will mission to put the Muslim League case to the United Nations General Assembly and the American public. She toured the USA for two months addressing meetings.

After Pakistan was created in August 1947 she became a member of the Pakistan Constituent Assembly. She served on four committees to draft the constitution. She worked for women's rights under the new constitution – not an easy task given the entrenched male prejudice in the committees. She also helped to frame the Charter of Women's Rights, a charter supported by all the women's groups in Pakistan. She campaigned hard to have it accepted by the Assembly and, in 1954, it was passed unanimously.

Begum Jahanara Shah Nawaz was bitterly disappointed that the constitution was abandoned when the Constituent Assembly was dissolved. After martial law was declared in 1956, she devoted her time to reading and writing.

Vijaya Lakshmi Pandit
Indian National Congress

Vijaya Lakshmi Pandit, as High Commissioner for India in 1955. In the 1920s and 1930s she played a key role in the Indian National Congress and the struggle for India's independence.

Vijaya Lakshmi Pandit, born in August 1900 in Allahabad, came from the wealthy middle-class Nehru family. She was brought up in a liberal, progressive household, where she was given the same freedom as her brother, Jawaharlal Nehru. Her father believed in the emancipation of women, and one of her cousins, Rameshwari Nehru, started a woman's magazine, *Stree Darpan* (the Woman's Mirror), which dealt with women's issues like property rights, education, divorce, remarriage of widows and the right to vote.

Vijaya Lakshmi Pandit was taught at home by an English governess. Her interest in politics began in 1916 during the Irish Rising when Terence MacSwiny, the Lord Mayor of Cork, went on hunger strike and died. She wrote an essay entitled 'The Memory of Terence MacSwiny's Death'.

She attended her first Congress session at the age of 16 at Lucknow. It was at this session that the Hindu–Muslim Unity Pact was signed.

With the emergence of Gandhi and the politics of non-cooperation, the Nehru family was increasingly drawn into the Indian National Congress. The family home became the centre of Congress activities in Allahabad, and for the next thirty years the family played a prominent part in India's struggle for freedom.

Like many other women, Vijaya Lakshmi Pandit was deeply influenced by Gandhi's ideas. After hearing Gandhi speak for the first time in Allahabad she was so moved by the message that, when an appeal was made for funds, she happily pulled off her gold bangles as a donation. When she got married to Ranjit Pandit she wore a homespun *sari* which she had dyed pink in the Kashmiri tradition. Instead of gold ornaments, she wore flowers.

During the *satyagraha* campaigns of the 1920s and 1930s, Vijaya Lakshmi Pandit, together with her sister, Krishna Hutheesing and sister-in-law, Kamala Nehru, joined the Congress volunteers. Her family took a lead in burning foreign clothes in public.

She was jailed three times. In January 1932 she was imprisoned in Lucknow Central Prison for a year for taking part in the Civil Disobedience campaign. In 1940 she was sent to Naini Central Prison. While in prison here she organised classes for the children of her fellow prisoners and for illiterate women. Her final arrest came in 1942, following the Quit India call. Because of ill-health, she was released after ten months. Her book, *Prison Days*, describes her experiences of jail life during her final term of imprisonment:

> Three or more police lorries were lined up on the road outside. In the darkness I could not make out the exact number. More armed men appeared out of the shadows. I was asked to get into the first lorry . . . Arriving at Naini I was informed that the jail authorities had not been intimated of my approaching arrival. Orders had apparently been communicated late at night to the police, and the jail staff did not expect me. After half an hour's wait, the door of the Female

Prison was opened . . . I was conducted to the old familiar barrack. It was 3.45 a.m. I spread my bedding on the ground, was locked in, and a new term of prison-life began.

Vijaya Lakshmi Pandit, Prison Days, *1945*

In 1935 she was elected to the Municipal District Board in Allahabad. She was appointed chairwoman of the Education Committee, initiating a milk scheme for the poor children of the municipal schools.

She contested the elections as a Congress candidate in 1937. Her constituency was the vast rural constituency of Kanpur, where she campaigned on the issue of self-rule. Everywhere her message was the same:

We told the people to repudiate the foreign government and to give their vote to Congress. 'Do you want things to remain as they are or do you want to have your own chosen people who will fight for your rights inside the Councils?'

Vijaya Lakshmi Pandit, The Scope of Happiness: A Personal Memoir, *1979*

Villagers flocked to vote for her and the Congress. She easily won against her wealthy opponent.

At the age of 37 she was made a Cabinet minister responsible for local self-government and medical and public health. She held the post till 1939; between 1946 and 1947 she held the same post again.

She was elected President of the AIWC and of the Save the Children Fund Committee between 1940 and 1942, when she did relief work during the Bengal famine of 1942. She also went on a tour of the USA, speaking at vast gatherings explaining to the Americans the reality of colonial rule. During the tour Vijaya Lakshmi Pandit made it a condition that she would not speak at venues where black Americans were not admitted.

In 1947 Vijaya Lakshmi Pandit became India's Ambassador, first to the USSR and then, in 1949, to the USA. She was amazed at the contrast in the Russian and American response to her as India's ambassador:

In Moscow I was *Gaspaja Pasol*, Madame Ambassador, and treated as such – no favours because I was a woman and no surprise that I was Ambassador . . . In Washington, however, I was Madame Pandit, Nehru's sister, and my being India's Ambassador was not taken seriously. It was an uphill struggle during the first few weeks to insist on this recognition . . .

Vijaya Lakshmi Pandit, The Scope of Happiness: A Personal Memoir, *1979*

In 1954 she became the first woman to be elected President of the United Nations General Assembly. In 1955 she came to London as the Indian High Commissioner – a post she held for seven years. On her return to India, she decided to become involved in Indian politics again and became governor of Bombay in 1964.

She died in 1990.

Timeline of main events

1885 Indian National Congress founded.
1901 Death of Queen Victoria.
Edward VII became King and Emperor of India.
1905 Bengal partitioned.
1906 Muslim League founded.
1909 Morley–Minto Reforms. Principle of separate electorates for Muslims established.
1910 George V became King and Emperor of India.
1911 Partition of Bengal reversed.
1914 First World War started.
1915 Gandhi returned to India from South Africa.
1916 Home Rule League set up by Annie Besant.
Hindu–Muslim Pact.
1917 Lord Montagu in India to investigate Indian claim to self-rule.
1918 End of the First World War.
1919 Government of India Act. Reform towards eventual self-government. Indians given responsibility for provincial government, Britain retaining control of central government.
Rowlatt Act. Repression.
Amritsar massacre.
1920 Gandhi began Non-cooperation Movement to achieve *swaraj*. Boycott of British imports and of British schools, courts and offices. Indians refused to pay taxes.
1922 Non-cooperation called off because of violence.

Gandhi imprisoned.
1928 Simon Commission in India to recommend whether India was ready for self-rule.
1930 Gandhi's march to Dandi to make salt. Civil Disobedience campaign begun. First Round Table Conference to formulate scheme for self-rule. Boycotted by Congress.
1931 Gandhi–Irwin Pact.
Second Round Table Conference. No agreement.
1932 Civil Disobedience resumed.
Third Round Table Conference. Communal Award. Each minority given a number of seats in the Legislatures elected on the basis of separate electorates.
1934 Jinnah became leader of Muslim League.
1935 Government of India Act. Provincial autonomy granted to the Indians.
1937 Provincial elections.
1939 Second World War started.
1940 Muslim League's call for 'Pakistan'.
1942 'Quit India' call by Gandhi.
Fall of Singapore to the Japanese.
Indian National Army formed.
1945 End of Second World War.
1946 Elections.
1947 Muslims launched Civil Disobedience campaign to demand an independent state of Pakistan.
Independence. India and Pakistan.

Glossary

ahimsa   non-violence

Bande Mataram   Hail Motherland

Begum   title for Muslim women

Brahmin   the priestly, or highest caste of Hindu society

chowki   lockup

dhoti   cotton wrap-around garment worn by men

harijans   literally 'blessed ones', or 'children of God'. Gandhi's name for the Untouchables, people outside the Hindu caste system

hartals   strikes and closure of shops

Inqilab Zindabad   Long live the revolution

jai   victory

khadi   homespun cloth

khilafat   anti-British movement among the Muslims in India after 1920

lathi   a wooden staff with metal tips at both ends

melas   fairs

phal-ahar   fruit meal

prabhat pheries   morning processions with chanting of hymns

purdah   veil

puja   a prayer ceremony, usually held in the home

rakhi-bandhan   tying of wristlets. Sisters usually do this to brothers

sanyasis   men who renounce the world, according to Hindu tradition

sari   woman's dress

satyagraha   literally 'truth persuasion' but commonly translated as passive resistance. Gandhi's policy of Civil Disobedience

swadeshi   home-produced

swaraj   self-rule

suttee   self-immolation of a widow on the funeral pyre of her husband

takli   distaff for spinning cotton or wool; spinning needle

thana   police station

zenana   women's quarters in the house. Upper- and middle-class women sometimes had their own quarters

Further reading

Background reference

Agnew, Vijay, *Elite Women in Indian Politics*, Vikas Publishing House, New Delhi, 1979

Ghosh, Niranjan, *Role of Women in the Freedom Movement in Bengal 1919–47*, Tamralipata Prakashani, Midnapore, 1988

Kaur, Manmohan, *Role of Women in the Freedom Movement 1857–1947*, Sterling Publishers Private Limited, Delhi, 1968

Mirza, Sarfaraz Hussain, *Muslim Women's Role in the Pakistan Movement*, Research Society of Pakistan, University of the Punjab, Lahore, 1969

Autobiographies

James and Margaret Cousins, *We Two Together*, Ganesh and Co, Madras, 1950

Begum Shaista S. Ikramullah, *From Purdah to Parliament*, The Crescent Press, London, 1963

Begum Jahanara Shah Nawaz, *Father and Daughter: a Political Autobiography*, Nigarishat, Lahore, 1971

Vijaya Lakshmi Pandit, *The Scope of Happiness: A Personal Memoir*, Weidenfeld and Nicolson, London, 1979

Vijaya Lakshmi Pandit, *Prison Days*, The Signet Press, Calcutta, 1945